Physics
of
God

Physics
of
God

Kartikey Singh

Vitasta

Vitasta Publishing Pvt. Ltd.
New Delhi

Published by
Renu Kaul Verma for
Vitasta Publishing Pvt. Ltd.
2/15, Ansari Road, Daryaganj,
New Delhi - 110 002

ISBN 10: 81-89766-26-0
ISBN 13: 978-81-89766-26-9

Typeset at Vitasta Publishing Pvt. Ltd.
Cover Design by Prabha Singh
Printed by Repro India Ltd., Mumbai

If I turn out to be particularly clear, you have probably misunderstood what I said.

Alan Greenspan

Contents

Acknowledgements

MY LIST for acknowledgements comprises one machine, one male, three females, a twin soul, my vagueness, a ghost and the God. It is helpful to make an inventory at the outset. You do not forget anyone.

One, machine…my computer; thank you. I have no acknowledgement more mechanical than this.

Two, my father…thanks for three reasons—(1) Along with my mother and God he has made me what I am; (2) He has made my fundamentally non-serious mind a bit otherwise; (3) He spent a lot of time in proof reading and correcting my poor English.

Three, my mother…thanks. No reason is required to thank her. She is the most important person to be thanked.

Four, my girlfriend…(probably she has married me)… for reading my first script and encouraging me throughout. I had to change almost the whole of my original script to make it more lucid and understandable to her. Then she could not get time to read it. I assume she will approve it as and when she will get time to read the book.

Five, my sister…for her irrational faith in my unknown capabilities. She thinks I can do anything. She wanted me to be a Bollywood star, a scientist, a poet and what not.

Against her standards I find myself spiritually and mentally malnourished daydreamer.

Six, my twin soul...my double powered soul who is the writer of this book. This acknowledgement is just for the sake of consistency as I have claimed inside that I am nothing but my conscious soul.

Seven, my vagueness...yes, my natural, elemental and foundational vagueness which prevented me from being clear on any issue. If you find me clear in thoughts anywhere in the book, it is just by mistake.

Eight, a ghost named Jampak Zu. He is our family ghost...harmless like any other ghost. He represents the combined voice of all who criticize my ideas. He is the co-author of this book in that he has also written his comments here and there in it.

Nine, the God...thanks for being the writer, reader, publisher of this book, for being this book...its ideas and material, for being the motivator and obstacles in writing, for being my teenage dreams, for being me and everybody around. Tell me, why this all damn delusion?

Ten, whosoever left and thinks himself or herself important to this book.

Jampak Zu Speaks

THANKS TO **K** (Kartikey) for giving me space in his book. I am just an observer of and commentator on the process, which was traversed by **K**'s mind in the making of this work. I am not a ghost as he has portrayed in the acknowledgements. I represent collective voice of all those who read the book and went against **K**, either seriously or non-seriously…and this includes **K**'s own voice which he suppressed. Despite all the pretensions of honesty, he has suppressed me to the extent of defeating my very purpose, reducing me into a meaningless intellectual joker.

Anyway, to bring a creature like God in the thin net of physics, even partly, is a difficult job. The hypothesis proposed in the book borders science and imagination. To me it seems a philosophical fiction. However, there is no credit to **K** but to his dreams in which he has no role. Why the great caravan of special cosmic dreams chose a mediocre mind to take rest is a puzzle that **K** himself does not know. Anyhow, the book is written after years of struggle dotted with despair and hope, moments of enlightenment and moments of realization of illusiveness of the former.

K has built up a strong and long runway from second to eighth chapters to give the final exposition of his thesis from ninth and tenth chapters. Such a long runway speaks of inefficiency of the engine of his aeroplane. However, you cannot skip runway of a flight, which is already prone to accidents.

K has no sense of humour. In his original script, he looked miserable on being humorous. Whenever he tried to jump down into the sea of humour, he always fell horizontally! Ultimately, he submitted and thus came this script...less non-sensical than before!

Introduction

*P*LACE: Allahabad, a peaceful city of India; TIME: Winter of 1991; CHARACTER: A simple college-going student; SUPPORTING CHARACTERS: None or probably God; HIS PRIMARY ACTIVITY: Night dreaming; SECONDARY ACTIVITY: Daydreaming; HOBBY: Thinking about dreams; PERIPHERAL ACTIVITY: Studies—this was me.

Initially, it all came to me as a vague dream...one after the other, night by night. It had poetic spontaneity, faceless beauty, rhythms of reason and awe of revelation. Those dreams were enlightening and confusing, pleasant and disturbing, meaningful and meaningless; at the same time. They were like streams of information that had probably lost their sequence and relational structures. Some were open, revealing and speaking while others were mysteriously closed, vague and like texts without context.

However, they were too heavy for a teenager to fully appreciate. I started jotting down these ideas but in a haphazard fashion. Every dream looked like a piece of jigsaw puzzle—connected yet unconnected. Time passed. They grew with me into youth. I started developing them into a single rational whole, after I entered the engineering college, joining them piece by piece. It became my favourite activity to think over them even when I was in the classroom.

By the end of my graduation, my ideas had grown into a loosely connected but so-called 'full-fledged model of cosmic reality'. However, it was full of conceptual blind spots and catches. In fact, my raw and virgin dreams, although confusing, were more beautiful than my self-acclaimed model based on them. At least, they had charm of cosmic mystery and beauty of suspense and uncertainty.

My so-called 'model of divine truth' had nothing except the mediocrity of judgments, haste of conclusions and ugliness of human reason. I myself was unable to consume what mess I had made out of those miraculous dreams I was blessed with years ago.

At one time, my ideas got entangled with so many problems that I started looking at them as rubbish and my teenage dreams as accident of intellectual romance. I was in need of some more similar dreams to clarify my problems and I got none. Probably, the teenage purity and innocence of my soul was no more with me to attract any more divine favour, if that was so. I see no other reason why God should not have helped me. When I took up my first job as a broadcast engineer, my ideas went into dormancy. A few more years passed.

Place: Lal Bahadur Shastri National Academy of Administration, Mussoorie; time: September 2003; my character: Probationer; other characterS: Other probationers; My primary activity: Adhering to schedule of academy; my secondary activity: Thinking on my model of reality while alone; my hobby: Well, no time for any hobby!

The real breakthrough in overcoming the conceptual problems occurred after I cleared Civil Services Examination in 2002. In the very first week after I joined Lal Bahadur Shastri National Academy of Administration, I suddenly and effortlessly solved a big conceptual snag in casual thinking. This revived my hope. [The problem was about the possible inter-relation of (human) consciousness and uncertainty of Heisenberg's theory].

Now, I restarted joining the pieces of my dreamy ideas with new vigour and in different ways. Time favoured this time. The jigsaw puzzle was solved almost completely and I, for the first time, was able to make out the complete picture of cosmic reality—the snapshots of which I had dreamt years ago. My teenager dream had become a complete man by now. I am indebted to room number 301 of Ganga Hostel in the Academy.

I cannot claim that I had cracked the truth of nature and God conclusively, but I was somewhat satisfied with my new model for I was able to preserve some charm of uncertainty and divine confusion this time! In the process, I realized that not everything could be left open to be scrutinized by the ugly reason of incompetent human mind. God cannot become crystal clear only by reason. It requires some divine help of revelation.

Well readers, if so, why to read this book? For wherever we find something indigestible or wrong in **K**'s thesis, we are incompetent human minds with ugly gray matter. So better put it back to vendor's shelf and go to meditate to get some revelation. If you get divine help, you will not need **K** and if you do not, **K** is of no help to you.

Jampak Zu

In the process of developing these ideas, I fell in love with physics and philosophy. Both the disciplines search for truth in their own way. Physics is natural science. It has objectivity and compelling verifiability. Philosophy is reason. It has subjective objectivity and compelling logicity. However, reason is dialectic. It always leads to its antithetical counterpart. So every philosophy has its anti-philosophy. This dialectics takes away the compulsion of logic and reason boils down to opinions. Hence, philosophy is not science though logical. Call it weakness of subject or charm, as you please.

Though I am fascinated by both the disciplines, their combination is deadly. It intoxicates me. The union of physics and philosophy is intellectually quite challenging and complex inter-discipline. It demands some knowledge of both to understand and appreciate. I have assumed that most of my readers either know only basic physics or basic philosophy or neither of the two. I have tried to keep its intellectual pitch suitable for all. Whatever physics is required has already been imbedded in simple and easy-to-understand package. So no specific academic background is prerequisite to read this book. It just requires common sense and aptitude.

I am not in a position to claim any certitude for whatever I am going to narrate in this book. The ideas and hypotheses therein come in the realm of speculative and rational knowledge, if it is knowledge at all. Their genesis lies in dreams and intuitions. There is no universality of experiences and no verifiability of experiments. They build upon the lack of certain knowledge. They rest on imperfections and limitations of the existing knowledge or thought system. They exist in possibility.

A hardcore positivist accepts any idea only if it is completely verifiable. However, this approach cocoons our quest for knowledge so much in the limits of verifiability that we forget to talk in the language of possibilities. We then only buy laws and never stop and stand at the stalls of hypotheses. This may stun our growth. The students of history of philosophy know how unsuccessful the positivist school of thought was. Positivist outlook can kill a budding idea on account of its imperfection. Ideas are organic entities. They take birth, grow or go ill and so on. If they die they reincarnate too. Positivist rejects what is unverifiable as un-verifiability is an imperfection in science. However, it is like rejecting a baby as complete human being for lack of teeth! Do not reject it—accept, give food and time, have patience before you find more and more perfection in the baby. The same is true for a 'baby idea'. Through this book I am giving you a baby to nurture. Can you help me?

ONE

Mystery of Reality
...Wondering the Obvious

...I in you or you in me...
He has told that I have the key;
Deep inside the mind and soul,
You are the part and I am the whole.

THE WHOLE nature that exists and plays around us is a puzzle. There are grand mountains, majestic rivers, thick forests, diverse flora and fauna, soil and rocks and twinkling stars from where fairies of tales come to amuse children.

The world is full of so many things, beautiful and otherwise. There are numberless celestial bodies, the stars, the planets, their moons, asteroids, nebula and what not; each having its own story, own history and own world. Most of them may not have life but they themselves seem to be manifestations of a greater and living cosmic scheme.

What all is this and why at all is this? Why there is a cool breeze or scorching sun? Why moon keeps revolving around the earth, the earth around the sun and sun around the centre of the Milky Way? Laws of gravitation narrate only the partial story. Why at all the earth has to be there to revolve around the sun? From where, has come this grand celestial structure? From where has come the material to make this structure? Who we are and what is our life made of? What is our identity? Are we more than our life or is our life more than us?

Do we know what life is? Are the molecules of our body, their combination in certain ways sufficient to produce life, or the flame of life is more than the matter and its molecules? If life is more than the matter and its molecules, from where has it come and from where has the matter come for that matter? What this matter actually is? Probably none of us know with certainty what matter is and the more lethal question: why it is?

One very amusing thing about this universe is that some portion of universe has capability to see and know about itself and also the other portion of the universe. I mean there are sentient beings like we humans having consciousness to perceive, conceive and understand the world around.

> *The most incomprehensible thing about the universe is that it is comprehensible*
>
> **Albert Einstein**

From where has this consciousness come in the structure of predominantly material universe? What is this consciousness made of? What is the locale of consciousness? Can there be a life without consciousness and consciousness without bodily life, or is life and consciousness one and the same thing? When we sleep, where does our consciousness go and then who sees the dreams? Where does our consciousness escape when we die?

I would like to talk about one small event from my life. Once I developed a very peculiar painful sensation in my feet. Initially, I avoided it only to aggravate the problem as it usually happens. I took some allopathic medication but that could not help. In fact, I believe that the doctor too was unable to understand my problem and was using trial and error method. Then someone advised me to take 'colours' from an acupressure specialist.

In colour therapy, colour dots or marks are put at specific points on hand. I took colours, with no faith in it, and in a day my problem disappeared. Specialists told me that there are ailments for which alternative systems of medicine are more effective. For me issue was not the system of medication but interaction of body-matter and colour.

Colour is neither conscious entity nor unconscious matter. If colour is a quality of matter, it makes no meaning to me. What do we understand by quality of matter? If matter and consciousness are two worlds, how does a quality go into consciousness? And if they can interact, what is the alchemy of that interaction? How they act upon each other? And how colour can treat an ailment of my material-physical body? How a quality of matter can make changes in the matter?

And who tells my body to respond to certain colours in a particular way? How one portion of universe knows how to respond to another portion of it? We usually classify the world in gross non-sentient matter and sentient consciousness; life and non-life. How does the consciousness, a non-matter, interact with and affects the unconscious matter?

Who has told all the honeybees, dead in past or living or yet to come in future, how to construct honeycomb?

How do all the cows know since birth that they should not eat non-vegetarian food? Who tells our genes to manifest certain qualities in a particular way? How and from where some innate ideas come to our mind since birth which we do not gather from any experience? Who gives us ideas of happiness, beauty and sorrow? Who teaches us how to smile and weep? Why something appears pleasant and the something else repelling? Who makes us fall in love? Who behind the curtain plays game with us?

Since my childhood, I am asking all these questions to myself. Someone said that asking is the very essence of growing. When we stop asking, we stop growing. On this account, my growth since my childhood has been tremendous. That my questions accumulated with no answer is a different matter. I feel we, the so-called grown ups, have been so much settled with the world around us and within that its existence is no more a puzzle to most of us. Our mind has compromised and accommodated with its incapacity to think deep into the puzzle of existence—it is philosophical what, why and how.

Pick up a particle of sand and try to contemplate upon it. It is a marvel of the whole universe combined. It requires infinite historicity of making and unmaking, innumerable forces from subatomic level to celestial one, matter of unknown origin and above all the creative randomness of processes which chiselled that sand particle into what it is today. It is a wonder. Everything is a wonder, a miracle, be it a growing bud, chirping of birds, laughter of kids or proverbial fall of Newton's apple. The knowledge of Newton's law of gravitation is no help to undo its wonder. It is rather a value addition to the miracle. Any law of science and nature that tries to explain any process or event only adds to its value as miracle for it shows that nature is following some pattern with no clue that who has authored these patterns and why.

Suppose there is an isolated gray stuff of human brain in a jar in suitable biological conditions that keep it alive. A scientist connects this brain with a computer through a wire and feeds all the data into it so that brain starts thinking that he is a boy in his room preparing for such and such examination. Data keyed into the brain can make it assume about the self-image of the boy, his parents, his lies, his friends, his likings and dislikings and his innumerable processes of daily life. This brain will actually think as we all think. Trust me, at least I do not hold any guarantee that the same is not the case with me. I am not sure that I do not happen to be just a pie of consciousness that is being fed with infinite details of life as data from the divine. The entire world may be just a database for mental consumption. Who knows?

Is existence real? Are the processes that occur in existence or fashion the existence like birth, death, love, sorrow real? When we say this or that to be real, do we understand fully what is 'real'? What is reality in itself? What is the nature and the character of reality? Have we ever found the reality per se or the source of its compelling existential authenticity and objective validity? NO, we only 'know' (we think we know) that this table or this earth or that man is real and so on. We then abstract a concept of reality from all these 'so-called' examples of reality.

Thus, our understanding of reality is a product of unconscious abstraction from the seemingly examples of reality. By perceiving the 'so-called' real things, we come to know what reality means. Such weak is the foundation of our understanding on reality that we ascribe something as real by assuming it as real in the very first instance. All of us are programmed to think like this. Who has programmed us for such mental symphony and how? For a moment suppose this entire world as an illusion—a mega-transcendental and universal illusion, which is always possible, then every object therein will be object of illusion. In that case, our understanding of reality abstracted from the existential status of worldly objects will turn out to be 'understanding of the illusion'!

Our understanding of reality does not go beyond the world, given to our consciousness. I could never understand and comprehend the character, locale, structure and logic of reality and real things (if there are such things) through simple perceptions.

There are confusions and puzzles at the level of philosophy and common sense and even at the linguistics level. If reality is something that exists in substance and is concrete, what is your opinion about the reality of someone's emotions? Are emotions and thoughts real things or are they even 'things' for that matter?

We may say that real is the one that exists, but it is like begging the question as we do not know what we mean by 'exist'. Even if granted that we understand the meaning of 'exist', dreams also exist, in our mind for some time at least. Are dreams real? Or are they semi-real? Can we find reality outside our consciousness, I mean outside the periphery of our consciousness?

Well, I must stop otherwise you may go crazy or you may feel that I have gone so. Human mind has devised/found (God knows which word is appropriate!) a grand key to all these connected questions. This key is God. God is answer to all questions.... He is the sum total of all answers. As concept at least, He is supposed to be.

However, the challenging corollary is that he is also the sum total of all questions and confusions. Due to infinitude, God, if He is, is beyond logic. Not by course of logic but by revelation, God renders all the answers to all the questions obvious. He obviates any further explanation, logic, proof or demonstrative knowledge. Those who have experienced revelation, if there are any, may tell better.

TWO

God
...The Uncertain Certainty

Fought with God...who is, who is not
Where is the figure when all is dot;
My chances of being real were bright,
If I could be in order to fight.

GOD HAS always been the point of ultimate reference or background of human thinking, knowledge and activities. Despite this, no one knows with certainty what He is or whether He really is. Throughout the flux of history, human wisdom by speculative reasoning and imaginative understanding has tried to penetrate deep into the philosophical what of God, through many ways. Hence, so many religions and species of metaphysics.

Does God really exist? This is probably the biggest question for mankind. Many thinkers have forwarded diverse testament for the existence of God throughout the recorded history of human thinking. These testament are based on the ontological, cosmological, teleological and even moral grounds. Those of you having little or no background of philosophy may feel uncomfortable with these terms. Let me brief them for you.

Ontological Proof

'*Ontos*' means essence. Ontological proof of God lie in deriving His existence as the very essence of the idea of

God. Essence of anything is the abstract and meaningful unity of qualities, which when combines with concrete, meaningless and discrete matter gives meaningful existence to that object. For example, flower-ness of a flower that is the unity of its beautiful qualities, meaning and the natural purpose is the essence of flower. The discrete molecular matter of flower becomes flower only when it combines with the essence of flower and manifests the latter.

Ontological proof starts with the *'idea of God'* that we have in our mind. We think of God as 'the most perfect conceivable being'. But if such a God that we think in our mind does not exist in reality, the idea of God will lack the *'quality of actual existence'*. Then it cannot be the idea of absolutely perfect conceivable being. As how can the idea of the most perfect being lack in the *'quality of actual existence'*?

The God that exists only in ideas cannot be the most perfect conceivable God! Hence, God must exist in reality. God can only be 'existing God'. Un-existing God is no God. Thus, the ontological argument says that the idea of God is so perfect that given that idea, His existence logically follows. If we can have idea of God as most perfect conceivable being, He must exist.

I do not know whether this brief illustration of ontological proof will be able to make any niche in your understanding. Anyway, rather than getting entangled here, better run through it.

Have you ever seen any author not intending the reader to understand what he has written? He is 'hit and fly' type of author. If it hits the reader, **K** is successful. If it misses, **K**'s main business is to fly! By the way, the biggest weakness of ontological proof is that it treats existence as a 'quality' to be possessed or not to be possessed

Jampak Zu

by an idea. Existence cannot be treated as quality. To provide nourishment is the quality of apple but we cannot imagine an apple and eat the apple of our ideas for calories. In fact, there are many versions of ontological proof and the finer ones are quite impressive but they all fall on the same ground.

Teleological Proof

'*Telos*' is a Greek word, which means end or purpose. Teleological proof indicates presence of God as the source of all purposes. For example, if there is a complicated organ like brain or eye in our body, there must be an intelligent designer who imputes purpose of thinking or seeing in the design of those organs. Such big and complicated but still harmonized world where all celestial movements, day-night cycle, cycle of seasons, etc., are so precisely synchronized cannot be an accident of evolution. It must have been designed by a mastermind—and that mastermind is God! Hence, God does exists.

Cosmological Proof

Cosmological proof for the existence of God points to an infinite and necessary being viz., God from empirical observation of the finite and contingent worldly beings. Roughly, this type of proof can be categorized in two classes. One is based on causal argument and the other on contingency argument. Causal argument says that every thing in this world has a cause which explains its existence. For example, a thing or event A is caused by another thing or event B that in turn is caused by another event C. Since everything is caused by another thing, in order to explain any phenomenon of this world, there will be infinite regress of causal chain. Take up any phenomenon and try to explain it.

The explanation will lead to many fundamental questions backward and every answer will generate more questions. Either this chain will disperse in many directions and continue or will come to a dead end where the issue will be elementally unanswerable. For example, if you want to explain the phenomenon of falling of apple from tree, you invoke another phenomenon viz., the gravitational force.

To explain the cause of gravitational force we may use the concept of time–space wrap. But physics stops here. If we go further to ask from where has time and space come from, science is of no help. Now we put our common sense to use and come with answers, which are nothing but opinions and even they give way to new questions that seem unanswerable. If our universe is all made up of the phenomena, which are ultimately inexplicable, the whole universe including own existence turns ultimately unexplainable. To render this universe explainable, which it must be, there must be a self caused and self explained being at the back of all worldly causal chains which is the source and cause of all things and event. This self caused and self explained being which must exist is God.

Contingency argument questions that why at all there should be things in the world or the world itself. Why there cannot be 'nothing'? What if there is no world? What if there is nothing? Are worldly things essential? Obviously not. Nothing in this world is logically essential. There is nothing which must exist.

Everything is contingent like a bubble in sea. Everything that exists can come and go, appear and disappear. The whole world is made up of contingent things. However, no contingent being can exist by itself. There must be a 'necessary being' as ground for all the contingent things to happen or occur. There must be a sea at base in order to have bubbles. This 'necessary being' that must exist is God. He is the substantive and essential base in which contingent and non-essential worldly things appear and disappear. Hence, God must exist.

You know philosophy is an art of answering a doubt with a bigger doubt. So it is always better to live with a philosophical question rather than a philosophical answer!

Jampak Zu

The above is just a very brief illustration of the various proof on existence of God. Actually, these proof are in much greater detail and full of philosophical technicalities and logical punch. Those who are interested in the subject may refer to some book on philosophy of religion.

Despite all efforts, the issue of whether the God exists is still unsettled. Every philosophy has its anti-thesis and every proof its anti-proof. A great German philosopher of modern age, Immanuel Kant, with all his sophisticated logic showed:

> *All the proof given for the existence of God are nothing more than opinions because no matter how powerful logic they may carry; an equally powerful logic can be given against them all.*

He said that God could at best be the matter of faith or belief. But hey Kant! Why only God? All the philosophies, logics and even sciences of the world are at the bottom a matter of opinion only. In his thesis known as 'Radical Empiricism', contemporary thinker Quine claimed:

> *No knowledge is absolutely certain.*

Some pieces of knowledge stand on firmer ground of wider observations and larger experimental evidences while others rest on smaller set of evidences and logical speculations. Hence, some knowledge seems more certain than the other. For example, observations of frontier modern physics about 'quarks' (particles which constitute protons and neutrons) or big bang may seem less certain than the observations about gravitational force of earth. This is because while there is wider set of observations and experimental support for the latter, there is leaner experimental confidence about quarks. In fact, today gravity looks like a settled fact of science, a piece of certain knowledge while the same is not true with quarks or big bang.

Thus, some knowledge seems more certain than the others. However, no knowledge is absolutely certain. It is all the matter of degree of certainty. To what we may think as absolute and infallible truth of nature may change tomorrow. Even the seemingly certain laws of gravitation and mass-energy conservation are all susceptible to change! That these are the truths of nature is just a matter of opinion. In fact, all the knowledge mankind has developed is based on experiences and opinions moulded out of them. These experiences may be direct observations or machine-aided observations (e.g., by telescope, microscope and spectroscope) or experiments.

After observation, some conceptual or mathematical model is developed to understand and comprehend what has been observed. This is the way how all the laws and theories of natural sciences are arrived at. We can never be sure that absolutely no error of observation or judgment creeps in the stage of experiment or theorization. It can be found only by some superior review. Since the possibility of superior experience or experiment which may demolish the older observation is always there, no piece of knowledge at any point of time can be said to be truly certain.

There were many laws and so-called 'facts' in science which were considered to be infallible and absolute at one point of time. There were logics and experimental evidences to support them. There were tall scientific authorities to assert them. They were considered the truths of nature. For example, mass and energy were considered as two different entities and there were separate laws of conservation of energy and mass. All the physics developed by Isaac Newton is based on this very notion that mass and energy are two different physical quantities that are separately conserved. Similarly, waves and particles were considered to be entirely different things with no mutual connection or intermixing. For example, electron was considered as pure particle revolving around the nucleus of an atom and rays of light were considered as pure [electromagnetic] waves.

Twentieth Century witnessed advent of Einstein's theory of relativity, notions of wave-particle duality advanced by de Broglie theory of wave mechanics and Heisenberg's uncertainty theory, etc. New physics proclaimed that mass and energy are one and the same physical quantity called 'mass-energy'.

Every piece of mass has or better say, is equivalent to some amount of energy and every quanta of energy is equivalent to some amount of mass. New physics also declared that every entity, every piece of 'mass-energy' possesses dual nature—nature of particle or lumpiness and nature of wave or patterned distributed-ness. No wave in this world is only wave and no particle is only particle. Every entity in this world has both the properties of wave and particle. Hence, electron revolving around the nucleus of an atom is not only a particle but also a wave. Similarly when we drive our car, we together with the car can be described as a group of waves moving in the direction of the car. On the other hand, the rays of light are not only waves but also beam of particles.

These new generation theories radically changed the whole conceptual bedrock on which the paradigm of conventional physics was resting. The old conventional physics of Newtonian age had its own set of conceptual frameworks, logics and experimental evidences and the new generation physics too has its own but different set of mathematics and experimental support.

The old physics had to give way to new physics only because the latter's experimental evidences and mathematics were far more superior and sophisticated than the former. If the absolute facts and laws of yesterday can be changed today; the best proved, the most sophisticated, the most logical and the most correct of today can also be demolished tomorrow by newer experiments, more advanced observations and even finer mathematics. So, there may not be any absolute and infallible piece of knowledge. Today's mind cannot guarantee that future mind will not think or find otherwise. Hence, every piece of today's knowledge is nothing more than an opinion on a larger timeframe and in bigger empirical perspective.

Now if we say that existence of God is a matter of belief but existence of this book is a certain fact or an electron revolving around the nucleus of an atom is certain knowledge, we will be labelling one belief as belief and the other belief as fact. To our surprise, all the matter made up of atoms may be illusion including we ourself. All our observations of this world, which make us believe in our surroundings we live in, may be illusion. I am not asserting that they are actually illusion but we cannot proclaim otherwise also. Who can assure with absolute guarantee that it is not so? As the guarantor, if any, He himself may be an illusion.

That we believe in what our senses tell us about the material world is ultimately a matter of choice. It is a belief that whatever we know through senses and mind must be correct. We only believe in our senses. From where did we get the certificate of correctness and authenticity of our senses, mind or this material world?

My purpose is not to make you feel that the world around is illusion. I only want you to open up your mind! Shed all sticky biases, if there are any. Know and eliminate hidden and implicit assumptions of your life and understanding and make them open and explicit. Realize that we actually believe in physics, no matter how rational and verifiable it is considered.

So let us make a humble start that whatever we know or we feel may turn wrong and illusive, and everything, every piece of knowledge and every concept is a belief at the bottom of epistemological critique. Some beliefs may be stronger and some may be weaker. Logic, mathematical models, experimental evidences, etc., only change the power a belief carries. No logic or empirical evidence can turn a belief into explicit, self-obvious, necessary and absolutely certain 'fact' or 'truth of nature'. This material world, as we see it, is as much a matter of belief as the existence of God. So suspend all your views about this world that you think are facts and write on your heart that anything you believe in may go right or wrong (or even may not go either way!) and same is true for what you reject or do not believe and also for what you might have never thought of.

Things are not what they seem to be, nor are they otherwise

Lankavatar Sutra

It is a belief that whatever we know through senses and mind must be correct. We only believe in our senses. From where did we get the certificate of correctness and authenticity of our senses, mind or this material world.

Today's mind cannot guarantee that future mind will not think or find otherwise.

No piece of knowledge at any point of time can be said to be truly certain.

THREE

Metaphysics
...The Unreasoned Reason

Here is the boarder of myths and the reason,
Where mind gets emotions and heart gets vision;
I see the oneness of the vague and the clear,
The flower of mystery has come to its season.

A LONG WITH God, there is also a big paraphernalia of ideas and concepts that are usually as powerful or as weak, in terms of logic, as the idea of God. This is called 'metaphysics'. Metaphysics is the whole set of ideas and concepts that are beyond the boundaries of the physical world and that cannot be captured in form of/through the lens of empirical evidences. We may say that as this material-physical world is dealt and understood by physics, any world beyond this physical world is 'metaphysical' and is dealt by metaphysics. Metaphysical world, if there is any, unlike physical world, is beyond direct and natural perception. Similarly metaphysics, if there is any such knowledge, unlike physics, is beyond experimental verification. Metaphysics is a creation of speculative reasoning by a philosophizing human mind. As per Kant's vocabulary, it is fabrication of rational faculties or 'categories' of mind.

Usually, God is the central idea of metaphysics but latter is more in span than the idea of God. For example, Hindu traditions claim that every human being is an immortal soul in a mortal body. When a body dies, the soul transmigrates from dead body to a new body and thus a new life is born. Now, this theory of transmigration of soul can be said to be a part of metaphysics of Hindu tradition. Similarly, all religions and many philosophies have their own metaphysics. Buddhism also has a huge structure of metaphysics with no God or say, Buddha Himself as the central idea. Plato's concepts of 'world of universal ideas' and 'logos' are also metaphysics (You need not know all of them to understand the point).

In the modern philosophy there is a school of thought called 'rationalism'. Rationalist philosophers believe in the capacity of human mind in finding the truths of nature that are beyond the direct human experience. They claim that by the use of reason (i.e., rational thinking) the un-experienced truths of nature can be discovered. So they apply reasons and logics step by step, speculate and build a mental construct or conceptual structure and then claim that the metaphysics of the nature is same as their own fabricated rational mental construct.

There is an underlying assumption that nature being the divine design itself must be logical and rational and the logic of its design must be in tune with the rational faculties of human mind. It is not a bad assumption as mind too is a part of nature or divinity and may have similar 'genetics of reason' that created the whole cosmos and its physical-metaphysical world. It means that the mind must think on similar lines, as the nature exists. A rational thinking must automatically be a reproduction, re-flash or re-traversing of divine design of nature. However, any claim with certitude is out of question here. Neither any certitude is sought for as stated in the beginning that to what we claim as certain knowledge vis-à-vis uncertain opinions may also go uncertain at the bottom of analysis. What I want to emphasize is that all the brands of metaphysics are fabrication of rational thinking. Metaphysics is a product of reason.

However, there is a 'paradox of reason' that intrigues me immensely. We know that reason and logic are always used to derive a new fact or idea from given facts, ideas and axioms. For example, if there are two triangles with same set of internal angles, reason can be used to show that the ratio of sides of both the triangles will be same. This rational conclusion is a universal truth. It is not a matter of opinion or belief. Students of geometry use reasoning to prove various theorems. The same is true for other disciplines.

In natural sciences too, we deduce various ideas and conclusions from some given piece of knowledge or experiment by reasoning it out. This is the natural way by which the mind explores the nature and subjects around and expands its share of knowledge. So reason is used to derive 'certain knowledge' from a given fact or some piece of knowledge. There can always be application of wrong reasons to arrive at wrong conclusions. However, the use of reason to derive new conclusions and thus to expand our knowledge and understanding of the world is undeniable. On the contrary, we cannot use 'belief' to derive any fact or certain knowledge. Belief, no matter how powerful it may be, cannot support the structures of knowledge. Reason carries logical coercive-ness (e.g., a theorem of geometry) while belief has emotive force and imaginative picture-ness (e.g., belief in angles). It means a rational conclusion (one found by applying reason) cannot be wished away or denied like a belief. A correct rational conclusion has universal applicability while belief is a matter of personal choice. Thus, 'reason' becomes definitional opposite of 'belief'.

However, the issue is not so straight. There is big overlap in reason and belief. If reason is logically coercive, it must be compulsive too. Ideally, it should not leave room for its anti-thesis or variant. But the case is just opposite when it comes to deal with a real or possibly a real thing or fact. What is this real or possibly real thing? The answer is—'anything which exist or has a potential to exist and which is not just a symbol or an abstract mathematical idea'. All the natural sciences and even metaphysics deal with real or possibly real things. These sciences and metaphysics have grown through application of reason on empirical observations and experiments. Their structure is built on reason.

First take the example of metaphysics. All types of metaphysics are products of reason. The metaphysical concepts, imageries and understandings are weaved by human brain through rational construction of ideas. The raw material or stimuli for metaphysical ideas may be empirical observations but our thinking mind goes beyond the visible facts and reasons out the constructs, which are not empirically obvious.

After observing birth and death of sentient beings, after recording the stray cases of people who seemingly remember their past life or any revealing observation, a human mind makes a construct of soul and theory of transmigration of soul. Irrespective of the truth or falsity, these are the rational constructs of meditation or reasoning mind. When we think of an angel or god with aura and supernatural powers and goodness, our mind creates a metaphysical imagery wherein mind reasons for overpowering goodness as purpose of this creation and puts it in an anthropomorphic cast.

Despite all metaphysics being just product of reason, no metaphysics is verifiably certain. We cannot verify the existence of angels or souls or give evidences beyond doubt for the transmigration of soul. Evidences, if there are any, can be only snapshots or glimpses in the domain of personal revelation, which can only be connected through reason. Neither are they complete nor universal. When somebody sees angels in dreams or even when awake, another person cannot penetrate into former's mind to claim it as evidence for existence of angels. Such experiences, if any, must be too personal for universal verification.

If metaphysical concepts are not verifiably certain or proved facts, we at the best can only believe it. Here comes the great paradox that a product of reason becomes a matter of belief. Actually, all the logical coercive-ness of reason lies within the territory of one species of reason. However, we always have freedom to subscribe one reason-species out of many (or even to choose none and stay unreasonable). This choice depends on what reason 'appeals' a particular mind the most. Hence, "belief in a reason or reason-product is a subjective choice and not a logical compulsion".

This paradox of reason (viz., product of reason or rational conclusion is ultimately a matter of opinion or belief) not only affects metaphysics but every other discipline of knowledge. We have already discussed that there is always the possibility of superior scientific experience or experiment which may demolish the older observation. Hence, no piece of knowledge at any point of time can be said to be truly certain.

The physics developed by Newton was well verifiable by the experiments of that time. His concepts were taken as perfect laws of nature. However, the rational constructs that originated in the mind of Newton turned out to be imperfect and just approximation of a more precise picture of physical reality developed by Einstein and then the founders of quantum mechanics. Today's physics is also experimentally verifiable but who knows the future. All our understanding of the physical nature can turn wrong despite huge progress of technology resting on this very understanding.

At any point of time, we only believe in the physics of that time with a faith that its theories will stand the test of time in future. They may or may not. Thus, despite all the rationality of physics, its infallibility and verifiability are not absolute. In physics, reason and belief coexist. The same is the case with every field of knowledge.

However, this co-existentiality of reason and belief is not present in mathematics! Take the same boring example: given the two triangles with same set of internal angles, it is a rational conclusion out of rational thinking that the ratio of sides of both the triangles will be same. It is a universal truth and not a matter of opinion or belief. There is no space for belief or faith in a theorem of geometry or arithmetic.

So why unlike metaphysics and other disciplines of knowledge like physics, 'paradox of reason' does not apply to mathematics? Any idea why? This is because mathematics is no knowledge!

So the student of mathematics! You are the student of no knowledge and mathematicians! You are big zeros. If you know how angels look like, you are knowledgeable. If you know how to solve a mathematical equation, you know nothing. This is what **K** wants to impress upon. Alas! And still you are reading him. Alas again!

Jampak Zu

You must note that mathematics including geometry never deals with the real facts, but only abstracts and ideas. Hence, it is only an analytical tool, not a natural science like physics. Triangle is not a fact but an abstract idea. So, a theorem of geometry related with triangles is not a piece of knowledge because it does not tell anything about any fact of nature. It is a mere tautology (repeating the same thing again). To have same set of internal angles in two triangles is same thing as having same ratio of their sides. The two things are not apart. Given one, the other necessarily follows. We may ask why this theorem is not a piece of knowledge. Let me take an easier example. Numbers are also abstract ideas. So 2+2 = 4 is also a tautology. Here, 2+2 is same as 4. It is like claiming x = x; which is obvious. There cannot be a world negating x = x or 2+2 = 4 or a theorem of geometry. It appears to be a piece of knowledge to us because our minds are finite.

To me numbers look more real and angel seems to be an abstract idea.

Jampak Zu

In our childhood, we were taught 2+2 = 4 and theorems of geometry. Our finite minds require training even to learn tautology. However, for an infinitely intelligent mind, say the mind of God, tautology is no knowledge. Hence, ultimately the whole Mathematics is no knowledge. It is only a set of abstract analytical tools of understanding. It only compensates for our lack of infinite intelligence. It is tool for knowledge and not knowledge by itself. However, Einstein's equation of mass-energy equivalence, $E = mc^2$ is a piece of knowledge as it tells some fact of this world. All tautologies are necessary as there can be no creation, no world and no right mind that can violate them, x = x and it will always be, come what may.

However, a fact or a piece of knowledge is never logically necessary. For example, there can be a world which violates $E = mc^2$ or theory of wave mechanics. So $E = mc^2$ or theory of wave mechanics are not logically necessary for this world to exist. So discovering them and knowing them as facts of nature adds to our knowledge. Hence unlike tautologies, they are worthy of being called 'pieces of knowledge'. The same is the case with metaphysics. It tries to find out the truths of nature using reason that are beyond the scope of normal physics. Hence, it is at least worthy of being called 'discipline of knowledge', from this point of view.

Students of history of philosophy know that the mid of 20th Century witnessed the rise of logical positivist school of thought. Logical positivism denounced the belief in metaphysics asserting that it is unverifiable. Its truth and falsity are equally unverifiable. Hence, metaphysics is not a legitimate subject of intellectual inquiry. Later on, logical positivism itself doomed as it was unable to give a simple, usable but perfect test of 'verifiability'. It may look simple to define what is verifiable and what not. But when positivist thinkers actually tried to pen down the litmus of verifiability, exceptions came to spoil the perfection of definition every time. At times, the strive for perfectionism overcomplicates things and becomes suicidal. In my exposition in this book, I will take all the care not to be perfect! Logical positivism appeals to me a lot. I fully agree with argument given by logical positivists that metaphysics is unverifiable, but I still stop short of denouncing it for two reasons:

One, all the knowledge is ultimately unverifiable. There cannot be any absolute verifiability for any piece of knowledge. Can the facts of physics be verified with absoluteness and finality? Can any amount of experiments do this? No, because had it been the case, once experimentally verified Newtonian physics should not have given way to new generation physics. In future, today's experimentally verified 'modern physics' may have to give way to some 'post-modern physics' based on entirely different conceptual paradigm and new set of experiments. So if we do not denounce physics for the lack of absolute verifiability, why to reject metaphysics for the want of verifiability? Accepted that metaphysics dealing with the world beyond this physical world does not have even preliminary or provisional verifiability which physics has but so what? Both are ultimately unverifiable.

Two, metaphysics, good or bad, sound or defective is but a reflection of the way human mind is destined to think. Rational speculation is the very nature of our thinking. We record some uniformity, pattern or system in the physical world, generalize them into laws and rules, extend them towards the realm of unknown and predict or speculate that way. For example, we observe that hot flames and hot shining lamps heat up the articles near by (observing a pattern). We then assume that all hot shining things heat up other objects (generalizing and making laws). We also see that sunshine too heats up objects (applying the law) and then conclude that Sun is also hot (extending to the realm of unknown and speculating). Thus, we come to know that the Sun is hot, though we have never directly touched it. No matter whether such a rational speculation comes true or not in a particular case, the development of knowledge through civilizational evolution is the result of this very pattern of thinking that dares to penetrate the unknown and even unknowable.

Hereby in this book, I am daring to unlock the reality of God and the whole creation that mystics enjoy, empiricists question, rationalists speculate, devotees believe, positivists reject and I...I claim...nay, "analytically believe in". Analytical belief looks a very balanced term to me. It is different from the religious belief of a devotee. It is rational, reasonable and at the same time acknowledges the contention of Kant and positivists that divine metaphysics being unverifiable can at the best only be a matter of belief or faith...

Metaphysics is a product of reason.

In physics, reason and belief coexist.

If we do not denounce physics for the lack of absolute verifiability, why to reject metaphysics for the want of verifiability.

Today's physics is also experimentally verifiable but who knows the future....
All our understanding of the physical nature can turn wrong despite huge progress of technology resting on this very understanding.

FOUR

My Approach
...Thinking About the Thinker

Who is the knower and what to be known
Who will show and what to be shown;
O sleeping consciousness! Wake up and think,
You on both the sides and you only the link.

*C*ONSCIOUSNESS IS the most obvious and living aspect of our existence and its presence as a part of universe can never be denied. It is at the back of all the eyes can see; the mind can think and the humanity can discern as the knowledge of science on the canvas of the physical world. It renders physics and every other natural science possible. It is so universal and essential to all the observations and knowledge that it should either occupy the first place in scientific disciplines or should have a science of its own.

However, its essentiality to the cosmic existence and the patterns in which it is weaved into universe are the issues which today no science deals with. I wonder why the compass of contemporary natural science is so small that it is unable to cover 'consciousnesses'.

If consciousness is the integral component and undeniable fact of the universe, why physics does not turn its eye towards it? Either the consciousness does not produce thrill of exploration in scientists or today's science feels helpless in front of it.

People travel to wonder,
At the heights of mountains,
At the huge waves of the sea,
At the long courses of rivers,
At the vast compass of the ocean,
At the circular motion of the stars;
And they pass by themselves
Without wondering.

St Augustine

Is it not a legitimate matter of inquiry for physics to know who is observing all the observations? Who is the real observer behind all the observations? Many scientific minds do not think so. For them, physics is meant for understanding objective aspects of nature while consciousness or conscious-self is the subjective aspect. Thus, the issue is left at the hands of psychology, philosophy or some yogic schools, etc. But to me, physics has now come to a stage where it must shake hands with the philosophy of consciousness if it aims to discover the cosmic reality in totality. Physics can never find the total truth of nature so long as it avoids its most prominent, most obvious and the most intriguing component. This venture of physics will also lift the subject of consciousness from the ground of obscurity. If we cannot expand the boundary of physics, at least this handshake is very much possible.

Our most inner being, our deepest self, is nothing but our consciousness. It is so transparent to any objective observation that we never realize it as an independent subject of inquiry. In every event of observation of a physical phenomenon or an object, our consciousness is intuitively so obvious and natural that it obviates any attention to itself. It keeps attention only on the phenomenon or object under observation. We always have consciousness of something i.e., a consciousness of consciousness engaged in something outside itself but very rarely have consciousness of our own consciousness only, which amounts to self-realization. However, a meditative mind can go beyond all the physical observations to feel the observing self. The deeper we sink into ourselves our consciousness progressively disengages itself from objective particularities of observation and rather engages with itself. This self-engagement, self-involvement or self-reflection of our conscious-self is the methodological tool with which we explore new realms of reality and existence.

Now here is the roadmap of how to go ahead in this book. First, I'll try to show that the realm of reality goes much beyond this physical world and there are many types of realities other than the physical reality. I will enlist and comprehend all these various types or levels of realities of which we are the parts. By logico-meditative introspection, we shall find that there are seven levels of realities constituting the cosmic existence and human existence participates in all of them. So man is a seven-fold being. As the beam of white light which when passes through a prism diffracts into seven fine lights of different colours making a spectrum, the light of all our objective and subjective observations and experiences combined when passes through the prism of introspection disintegrates into seven levels of reality. In this task, I will take help from some Indian philosophical schools, theosophy and above all from everything that we can gather from our own inner self-reflection and consciousness. Internal reflection is the great source of knowledge. I may be under illusion of achievement but I was surprised to see that by contemplation, by mere thinking and serious introspection, I was able to thread bear my own conscious-self! Both the process and results are simple but still intriguing. You may find that the total reality is only little amount of material world and rest all is of your own consciousness!

After finding various levels of reality, we shall proceed to synthesize them according to some pattern and build a general picture of all that exists or the 'integrated system of reality'. This general system of reality will subsume all the realities...

a. that we reach at objectively (i.e., reality of physical object which we perceive by our senses and mind) and
b. all inner subjective reality that reaches at something objectively (e.g., reality of self-consciousness which perceives objects objectively)

The physical reality will be woven in this general system of reality according to a certain pattern. For this, I shall investigate and record the sensible (observable by senses) and physically verifiable facts and laws belonging to the physical reality. These facts and laws shall then be speculatively and rationally extended to other levels of reality according to some pattern. This means application of laws of physical world to other levels of reality for which no law is known to us—extending laws of known domain to the realm of unknown. This extension or generalization of laws rests on the assumption that physical reality being one aspect or level or particular case of cosmic reality (integrated system of reality) must have a genetics of reasons and structures that is common to other levels of reality too. This is like making of metaphysics on the lines of physics.

The most challenging part of this project is to find that pattern or common genetics of reasons on the basis of which the fact and laws of physical world will be extended to other levels of reality...and the physical will be generalized as metaphysical! I shall then try to uncover and comprehend the existential and objective meaning of all realities including the ultimate reality that is God. To my surprise, the reality of God reveals itself automatically at the culmination of my analysis. The proposed road map may appear vague at this moment but it will become clearer as it unfolds itself.

The realm of reality goes much beyond this physical world and there are many types of realities other than the physical reality.

The most challenging part is to find that pattern or common genetics of reasons on the basis of which the fact and laws of physical world will be extended to other levels of reality.

FIVE

Reflections on Consciousness
...Discovering the Obvious

Layers after layers in the inner space,
Run after yourself if you can chase;
To stop at a point when you are caught,
Only to find that here you are not.

A S A new born child opens his eyes the first scene that he comes across is of sensible objects…chairs, tables, lamps, bodies of other human beings and so on.

Physical Reality

This physical world is the first taste of reality a human mind may experience. This primal experience of physical reality is the basis of our understanding about what reality is. Whatever we experience or perceive is naturally accorded an independent objective existential validity by our faculty of understanding. This means that when we observe a physical object, say a flower by our senses, we do not simply observe the design, colour, softness and odour of the flower as mere discrete sense data entering into mind from a mysterious source; we rather cognize the flower as really existing. To our perceiving mind, a flower is not merely 'design-colour-softness-odour' put together but a mixture of its qualities in an unknown, mysterious crucible. We perceive it as a substance, a thing and a reality having all these qualities. Our mental faculties are programmed to assume that something actually exists corresponding to the sense data we receive.

This reality of physical world 'as is perceived by human mind' has a character of its own. This character is so obvious for us that its illustration may be boring. Still I would like to summarize it in a few points:

1. There are numberless physical objects of limitless variety. From tiny particles of dust or pollen grains to tennis balls, tables, chairs, human bodies, the moon and stars, whatever we see, are physical objects. The surf at the seashore is made of molecules of water. Sunshine is made of photons and the particles of light. Smoke from fire is nothing but molecules of un-burnt gases and vapour. Fire is made of highly ionized atoms. They all are physical objects, bodies or particles. We do not see anything other than physical objects or their combinations in this world.

2. Every physical object has its own kinematics (motion-rest). For example, there are cars and rockets moving in space-time, houses and furniture seemingly at rest, particles of dust bubbling and bouncing in random directions (as we see when sun or torchlight passes a dusty room), drops of rain running down to earth from sky. They all are perceived to be situated in a space-time reference or continua and thus fill the latter. Can we imagine a world without these moving or resting physical objects? That must have been an insipid and boring world with barren stretch of space and event-less beat of time and nothing else.

3. There is another peculiar character of this physical

world. Here, we find that physical objects are devoid of consciousness. However, we may question this point as human bodies do have consciousness. To me, physical object is a pure material entity. Human body, as we will find in coming pages, is a complex of a body of matter and various types of consciousness. A human mind can be logically analysed into brain cells made of matter and a subtle and non-material mental consciousness. Here, only the first part viz., material brain is worthy of being called physical object and not the unperceivable consciousness associated with it. Similar logic works for the entire animate world.

However, the claim that physical objects are devoid of consciousness is only an inferential conclusion based on symptotic analogies. We generalize our consciousness with animate world, find a general notion of what consciousness is on the basis of symptoms, compare the inanimate world with animate world and conclude that inanimate or physical world has no consciousness. As we cannot see consciousness directly, we can never assert with absolute certainty about what is conscious and what is not (in fact, theosophy and every other school of thought which believes in the concept of 'monads' attributes some primal level of consciousness to matter as well). In this book, I will attribute zero consciousness to physical reality just on common sensical basis. This axiom is humbly provisional.

To my senses and mind, this physical world is all real. It is the first and the most obvious example of reality that educates our minds about what reality is. This reality, as we discussed, has its own character. We shall see that there may be other types of realities as well with entirely different character. Hence, I look at this physical reality only as a type of reality...just one among many types and the physical world as a 'level of reality'. In theosophy, this level is called *Bhu lok*. In Sanskrit, *lok* means 'world' and *bhu* means 'earth'.

Non-physical Reality

When we reflect back into our own consciousness, we find some other types of realities. Our consciousness is something which *"is"*.... It exists. Its presence is subjectively obvious. Its reality is undeniable. Hence, we can take it as another type of reality different from the physical reality that is devoid of consciousness. Let us analyse and investigate what we call our consciousness. We will find in the coming pages that our consciousness as a whole is not a single monolithic non-physical reality but a complex of multiple types of non-physical realities.

Consciousness is the basis of cognition, knowing, understanding, thinking, feeling, etc. It is very difficult to give a precise definition of consciousness. It is the basic principle and essence of knowledge.

One cannot know anything without consciousness. Consciousness in us is the ultimate knower. We may better say that who knows is consciousness. If I am seeing a flower, it is who, who is seeing the flower? Can all the cells of my eyes and brain together see and know the flower? The answer is 'No'. Since same cells are present in an undecomposed dead body also.

Even if we pump blood in brain and eyes of a fresh dead body by life-saving machines, we can never be sure that the eyes and the brain are actually seeing the flower, and even if they are seeing, it is who, who is knowing that there is a flower? There is no one! There is no conscious principle in the dead body. Dead body is just like any stone, rock or sandbag. It is only our consciousness *who* knows. If I say that I see and know that there is a flower, it means that I am nothing but consciousness. To what I call 'I' or my conscious selfhood is nothing but consciousness.

Consciousness is the living principle of cognition. Cognition means perceiving something and conceiving it. We shall see that cognition is popularly understood as a two-step process. The first step of cognition is 'sensation' viz., reception of sense data of colour, touch, smell, sound, taste, etc., by sense organs and its communication to brain.

Hence, though sense organs themselves are physical, being made up of matter, their potentiality of experiencing sensation can be taken as a non-physical type of reality because this sensation is the primal manifestation of consciousness. Receptivity and sensibility of sense data of colour, taste, smell, sound and touch by sense organs shows that these physical organs must be repositories of some form of consciousness. We may call this 'sense-level consciousness.'

Thus, as the hardware of senses or the sense organs is physical reality, 'sense-level consciousness' or the software of senses, as we may call it, is real despite being beyond the physical world. It is a type of non-physical reality…a different level of reality overlaid or superimposed on the physical level. Roughly, it is this second level of reality having some form of consciousness that corresponds to *Bhuvar lok* or 'astral world' in theosophy.

Mental Consciousness

We may now proceed to a higher level of consciousness. In the process of cognition, the sense data as received by senses is synthesized, cognized and understood. It must be done by a higher level of consciousness…higher and more refined than level of senses. Repository of this higher level of consciousness is mind. Many philosophical schools, oriental or occidental, recognize the fact that cognition is a two-stage process. Its first step involves merely reception of crude sense data by sense organs. As per Kant's vocabulary, it is 'perception without conception'. Nyaya school, one of the six orthodox traditions of Indian philosophy, names it *nirvikalpa praman* viz., 'sensation of a thing as such without understanding what it is'. The second step or part of cognition is understanding and recognizing what has been sensed. Nyaya calls it *savikalpa praman* i.e., 'perception with conception'. These two aspects or steps of cognition are not separate in actual cognition but are simply the product of logical analysis of any valid and meaningful cognition.

Sensation is the function of sense organs while conception or understanding is the function of mind. Since the latter requires the synthesis of received sense data in particular pattern and context and then understanding of the virtually synthesized object or idea, the mind must have a consciousness much higher in degree and quality than that of sense organs. The mental consciousness must also be active and synthesizing in nature unlike consciousness of sense organs that only passively and discretely receives the sense data. This consciousness possessed and represented by mind constitutes another level of reality. It must be noted that the reality of mental consciousness does not encompass the physical brain made of cells, as it is merely a physical reality.

In theosophy, the reality of mental consciousness constitutes a world of its own that is called *Manomaya lok* or 'plane-of-mental-body' or *Manas*. This is the third level of reality.

Consciousness of 'I-ness'

Now we should analyse this mental consciousness to extract the even finer residue or the even higher level of consciousness, if there is any.

Our mental consciousness to which the functions of cognition, conception and understanding have been attributed is 'intentional and objective' in nature. The word 'intentional' as used by phenomenologists like Husserl and existentialists like Sartre is typical and technical in philosophical literatures. It means that consciousness as we possess in mind is always 'consciousness of something' rather than being 'consciousness as such' or 'consciousness-in-itself'. We always have consciousness of external (to mind) physical objects or objective internal mental feelings, e.g., consciousness of table, chair, pain and pleasure. We always have 'consciousness of'…and not simply consciousness… the barren stretch of consciousness.

This intentionality of mental consciousness is manifested in the objectivity of human mind and thinking. If we reflect upon our cognitive process, we find that human intellect is destined to approach anything physical or mental as an object. Let us imagine a visual construct of an arrow or vector with tail pegged at centre of a circle. This arrow is like our mental consciousness and the circle in which this arrow sweeps likens the field of cognition. All the mental objects (ideas, feeling etc.) and images of physical objects stand in the field of cognition to be cognized and comprehended.

Our mental consciousness is objectively programmed to captures these objects. It points to an object of cognition in the same way as our finger points to some object. The tail of the vector of mental consciousness denotes our inner self. As our finger despite being capable of pointing everything and touching the thing that it points, cannot point to or touch its own tip, the mental consciousness being intentional and objective cannot capture its own inner being objectively.

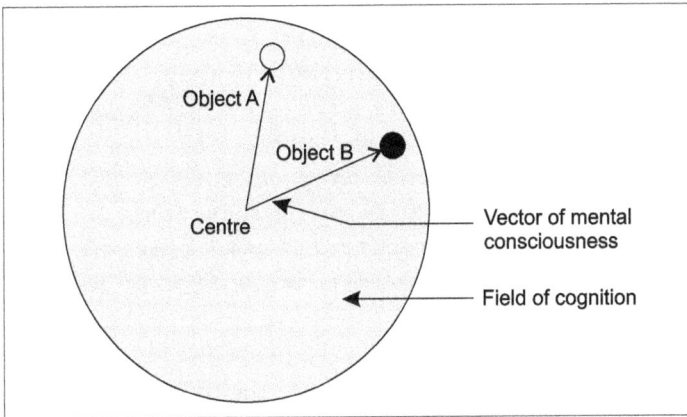

Fig. 5.1   Object and Objectivity

That means the subjectivity of human mind cannot be reached at objectively. It can only be done by switching off or annihilation of the outward looking consciousness... that means withdrawing the mental consciousness from out-worldly objective engagements and sinking into self and gravitating within. Pictorially, it is like shrinking the length of vector of mental consciousness to zero so that tip of vector may touch its root.

Futility of catching the mind or mental consciousness objectively is beautifully worded by David Hume:

When I enter intimately into what I call myself, I always stumble on some particular perception or other, of heat or cold, light or shade, love or hatred, pain or pleasure. I never catch myself, at anytime, without a perception and never can observe anything but the perception.

Hume further coments:

Mind is a bundle or collection of different perceptions which succeed one another with an inconceivable rapidity and are in a perpetual flux and movement. The mind is a kind of theatre where several perceptions successively make their appearance, pass, repass, glide away and mingle in an infinite variety of postures and situations. There is no simplicity in it at one time, no identity in different [times].

However, we can capture only the scenes of perceptions of external-internal objects and not the theatre where they are presented i.e., our own mind. As per Hume, we are not sure about the locale of this theatre or even about the fact whether any such theatre (mind) really exists. All this shows the helplessness of capturing our inner subjectivity with objective intellect.

Here, I am interested in finding the significance of intentionality and objectivity of mental consciousness in the context of our general analysis of consciousness. Our mental consciousness is always consciousness of something. Let us compare the consciousness of a table with that of a chair. Here, table and chair are referred to as some particular ones and not general class of table and chair. What is different in these two events of consciousness or cognition is only the object or say, content of cognition.... And what is common? Common is the subjective end of intentional consciousness viz., 'I'. There are say two events of cognition:

Perception 1: I perceive table.
Perception 2: I perceive chair.

When I perceive table or chair, I essentially also perceive that I perceive. Hence in every event of perception, there is a perceiving 'I', different from the object of perception. In Perception 1, the object of perception is table while in Perception 2, it is chair.

However, 'I' as the perceiver is common to both. This 'I' stands as essential background of all cognition/ understanding or intentional consciousness. It allows the latter become possible.

Notably, 'I' is not the faculty of synthesizing any data and understanding any object-image or idea. It is the inherent and silent appendage or prerequisite to understanding. When I have consciousness of some object or idea, I at the same time must have an implicit, silent and continuous consciousness of 'self' or 'I-ness', which is different from the object/idea or consciousness of it.

This consciousness of 'I-ness' is the logical and psychical presupposition or precondition of any mental consciousness. Consciousness of table or chair points back to someone or something who is conscious…who is bearing a particular mental consciousness (of table/chair/idea).

This consciousness of 'I-ness' is also called 'ego' or '*aham*'. It is the consciousness of self as 'me' and has nothing to do with common sensical usage of the word 'ego' as a characteristic of personality. When someone says, 'He has a lot of ego. It is difficult to deal with him,' one is referring to a characteristic of somebody's personality or behaviour.

The consciousness of 'I-ness' is entirely different. It is a level of consciousness, a reality in its own right, a layer of inner subjective existence of human being. To differentiate it from common usage of the word 'ego', this consciousness may also be called 'spiritual-ego'. It is more refined and higher than the general mental consciousness because mental consciousness is intentional, engaging and has a variety while the consciousness of 'I-ness' is 'unintentional-in-itself'...being at the subjective end of intentionality, 'unengaged-in-itself', one and continuous.

Amidst the variety and flux of mental cognitions, the consciousness of 'I-ness' provides the required higher unity of apperception and inner continuity of sameness of the observer. It provides me with the subjective identity that I am the same observer who had seen the table and who perceives the chair now.

Referring to Figure 5.1, the 'I-ness' likens the centre of circle from where founts the vectors of mental consciousness. Hence, 'I-ness' is an implicit presupposition or prerequisite to my mind or mental consciousness.

This consciousness of 'I-ness' can be taken as another level of consciousness and reality, which is above the level of reality of mental consciousness. This reality of 'I-ness' constitutes a world of its own which may correspond to *Vijyanmay lok* or 'Plane-of-Spiritual-Ego' as described in theosophy and many oriental literatures.

The consciousness of 'I-ness' or ego is my identification to myself, my self-authentication to my valid existence. This

'I-ness' is connected with the person that I am. It is beyond my body, beyond my mind, but is connected to both. It is my first and elemental introduction to myself. Perhaps, Strawson in his 'Theory of Person' is correct to the extent he asserts, 'I am more fundamental than both my body and mind. My elemental ego or 'I' that defines my being is prior to my mind. I am primary, my mental consciousness is secondary.' It is logically correct too. First there must be 'I' to claim that there is something, which is mine, e.g., 'my' mental consciousness. Well, but this 'I-ness' is uniquely connected to my mind, senses and body. For example, my consciousness of 'I-ness' is connected to my body, senses and mind and giving rise to my person-hood who is named 'Kartikey' in a group of other persons like me.

One thing I would like to add is the significance of word *Vijyanmay lok* as used at many places in ancient literatures. Some schools of philosophy rightly put *budhhi* or *prajya* or intellect above mind while giving catalogue of nature. Word *Vijyanmay* means something carrying or loaded with intellect. It is not the mental consciousness but the spiritual ego that is repository of intellect. The structures of mental consciousness are too fleeting and ever changing to constitute intellect. Hence the world of systems, which constitute consciousness of spiritual ego or 'I-ness' is called *Vijyanmaya kosh*.

Jampak Zu

Consciousness of 'Pure-I'

Let us dare to further analyse the consciousness of 'I-ness' to see if there is any finer residue in it…even finer than the consciousness of 'I-ness' or spiritual ego. My consciousness of 'I-ness' or ego is my subjective identity as a person. My spiritual ego or 'I-ness' encumbered with my body, senses and mind represents my unique person-hood. However, what will happen if this consciousness of 'I-ness' is stripped of all the external self-identifying qualifiers or encumbrances of person-ness?

If my consciousness of 'I-ness' is stripped of all the qualifiers that are unique and particular to Kartikey i.e., my body, my senses, my mind, my self identification as a knower of the worldly objects and ideas and bearer of my person-hood, what remains is the bare 'I' which is 'I but not Kartikey'. It is just an individual quantum of pure consciousness uncontaminated by my person-hood. Since it is free from the encumbrances of person-hood or particular-ness of Kartikey, logically it is possible that Kartikey may die but 'pure-I' may not.

Every event of cognition is like a perturbation in mental consciousness by the sense data which fashions or engages 'I-ness' or ego or *aham* and thus my *aham* realizes that I am cognizing something. Hence, *aham* is engaged in all the events of cognition as a psychical background which provides a subjective identity to the observer. On the other hand, 'pure-I' remains unengaged and unaffected in events of cognition. 'Pure-I' remains still, unconnected and an undisturbed observer. This 'pure-I' is also called *atman* or soul. It is a self without self-ness. According to the theory of transmigration of soul, every creature has a soul that owns a 'body-sense-mind package' in physical birth and leaves it during physical death. What dies is that package and not the soul. The same soul goes through a series of owning-disowning events of 'body-sense-mind package' that is explained as birth-death and rebirth of creature. Many religions have some or the other versions of the concept of soul and its immortality.

Notably, the theory of transmigration of soul and its immortality are not verified or verifiable as theories of natural science. However, the concept of immortality of soul fits well in my present model of multi-layered reality that I am attempting to structure through logical and psychical analysis of human consciousness.

'Pure-I' or *atman* or soul is the bare individual consciousness free from all encumbrances of person-ness or particularized 'I-ness' that limits me as an individual knower (having mind) of some object or idea at a particular space and time. This 'pure-I' is a different level of reality ...higher and more refined than the reality of ego or 'I-ness'. World of reality constituted by 'pure-I' corresponds with *Atman lok* or *Anandamay lok* of theosophy.

Here, death merely means the dissolution or decomposition of any assembly or package into its elements. As in the physical world, there are elements and a human body on death decays in those physical elements;

we may assume that there exist elemental components, analogous to particles of the physical world, in each level of reality. In every world, birth means certain combination of basic elements or particles of reality (corresponding to that world) and death or decay means dissolution of that combination, back to the basic elements. This is just a conceptual pattern. Word 'particle' as used for every world or level of reality should not be confused with the notion of physical or geometric particle as it stands in physical world or Euclidian space. Particle simply means 'basic elements of reality of a particular world'. What they are, how they are like, we do not, need not and possibly cannot know.

Pure Consciousness

Now a question arises–what will remain if the consciousness of 'pure-I' (or soul) is stripped of the very 'I' itself?... Let us understand the question again...not an easy question please. Suppose I am conscious of 'I', the 'pure-I', my deepest self, the soul that I am – free from any physical-mental-psychical qualifier or encumbrance of ego or person-hood. This 'I' is free from Kartikey-ness – my person-ness. It is immortal. It has owned Kartikey-ness for some time in undetached manner. If we accept the theory of transmigration of soul this 'I' will continue even when Kartikey will die.

Though the 'pure-I' or my soul or *atman* is free and immortal; it is limited and determined because it is 'I'. It cannot be more than 'I'. It cannot go beyond 'I'. It cannot be you! Now, let us repeat the question: what will happen if consciousness of 'pure-I' (*atman* or soul) is stripped of this limitations of the 'I' itself?... What will remain is pure consciousness, consciousness-in-itself with no individuality, no boundary, no determination, and no limitation.... That will be limitless, boundary-less and indeterminate consciousness.

Every soul or *atman* is an individual and individuality by default brings determination, limitation and finitude. However, pure consciousness without the individual 'I' is essentially infinite and unbound consciousness. At this level of reality, all the individualities convulse to become one and the same thing which is conscious...undivided, undetermined and unlimited. It is all inclusive consciousness .... No one of us is out of it, no one is other than it. The pure consciousness is the supra-individuality subsuming all that is sentient. My individual soul that I am is my pie of consciousness in the infinite and universal reservoir of pure consciousness. This world of pure consciousness is the highest level of reality which is further unanalysable either logically or psychologically. In theosophy, this is called *Adi lok*.

Pure consciousness is the ultimate reality from which founts all the light of sentient existence. It increasingly gets contaminated by determinations and limitations of individuality (seen as soul), by attributes and qualifiers of person-hood (ego), by functions of cognition and thinking (mind) and sensing (senses) as this light percolates to lower worlds. Thus the one, pure, undivided, unlimited, undetermined and unqualified absolute reality manifests itself into lower levels of reality that are impure, multiple, divided, limited, determined and qualified.

Reality of God

There is one more level of reality to bring out. Through step-by-step logico-psychical analysis of human consciousness, we have captured six levels of realities up to this point. Out of them only five are the levels of sentient realities viz., senses, mind, ego, soul and pure consciousness.

As per our common sense assumption, the physical world having zero consciousness is non-sentient. However, we know it through consciousness only. We know only that physical world as we see it through senses i.e., which lends itself to human understanding in form of sense data and mental images. We never know the physical-world-in-itself. We only see the sense data of a table or a chair. What is the source of this data, our intellect actually never knows. In terms of Kant:

> *We never know the 'things-in-themselves'. We only know perceptions and nothing beyond perceptions.*

Having said this, let us explore the question—'Can human consciousness know or capture pure consciousness?' Human consciousness can know and capture pure consciousness only if the former has complete perception of the latter. However, human consciousness is limited and finite. It has no independent existence as it founts from pure consciousness only, which is infinite and limitless and is the ultimate source of all consciousness of the universe. Just as a finite vessel cannot contain an infinite substance, a limited and finite human consciousness cannot comprehend and fully capture the infinite pure consciousness. Human intellect cannot have the perception of infinitude. So the answer to the question is in negative.

Now a question arises—'Given that finite human consciousness that cannot perceive infinitude of pure consciousness; if the former tries to introspectively perceive the latter, what will it actually perceive?'... A finite consciousness can only see, imagine or comprehend the finite. So human consciousness will perceive only finite, symbolic and fractured snapshots of pure consciousness. Humanity calls it God! God is pure consciousness as conceived, understood and captured by limited human intellect...finite snapshot of the infinite.

The difference between pure consciousness and God is only of human cognition. Mind cannot capture the limitlessness and indetermination of pure consciousness and hence can conceive it only as determined and limited. Hence, God as conceived and worshipped by human mind is bound to be qualified, determined, finite and limited (no matter how intensely the mind thinks about the limitlessness of God and the tongue utters the same). Thus, the ultimate and unqualified reality renders itself in qualified reality.

This qualified and finite reality of God constitutes a world of its own which is below the *Adi lok* of pure consciousness but above the *Atman lok* of 'pure-I' or soul.

This may roughly correspond to what is called *Anupadak lok* in theosophy.

Gordon Kaufman in his *God the Problem* has distinguished between the 'real God' and the 'available God'. Here, real God corresponds to pure consciousness and available God is the one, who is available to human understanding i.e., manifestation of ultimate reality as it lends itself to human mental consciousness. Shankaracharya, the great Indian philosopher and profounder of *Advaita Vedanta* school of thought differentiates between *Brahma* and *Ishwar*. *Brahma* for Shankaracharya is pure consciousness and *Ishwar* is God as understood and worshipped by human minds.

If soul is an individual pie in infinite consciousness and God is the finite snapshot of it, we may have the idea of God as 'super soul'…conscious entity, which may be overwhelming and grand for an individual soul but still having form and finitude unlike infinite pure consciousness.

There is one question, which has potential to trigger chain reaction of philosophical arguments…. If available God and its world is nothing but pure consciousness as captured and conceived by human intellect, it means the world of available God is nothing but illusion or appearance to human intellect. Can we call it a real world? Is the God as we know him unreal?..smart question…. It was asked to me by one of my friends. Lord Buddha might have answered it with his telling and mystical silence. I do not have such charm in my silence…. I tend to speak…small creature.

Actually, pure consciousness is the only absolute reality. All other levels of reality including that of God are its successively diminishing appearances. Hence all realities, except pure consciousness, are ultimately delusion including the God *as we know Him*. The reality of this second level i.e., available God, when manifests itself in multitude of individual souls, then appears the third level of reality viz., the world of soul(s) or 'pure-I'. When a soul owns 'body-sense-mind package' [in birth], a person-hood comes into being.

The 'pure-I' encumbered with this person-hood, manifests itself as consciousness of 'I-ness' or ego or *aham* causing the next lower level of reality to appear. Ego manifests its existence through and in numerous events of mental cognition, which correspond to the reality of mental consciousness. Mental consciousness is like ongoing contingent perturbations or ripples on a constant ground of ego. It varies with different cognitions just like making and un-making of bubbles at the surface of the sea water.

The light of mental consciousness diversifies itself into many types of sense consciousness. Sense consciousness is primal and the lowest form of consciousness, which is only capable of receiving sense data. One event of mental cognition involves myriad events of sense consciousness weaved into some understandable pattern by mind. A flower cognized by mind is a combination of consciousness of its colour, design, texture, odour, distances etc.

At last, comes the lowest form of reality viz., physical reality comprising objects of the physical world such as table, chair and tennis ball as seen. We do not know the source and essence of all these things. We do not know whether they are just bubbles or forms in the field of consciousness or something independent of consciousness. Even Kant does not know. If we do not know anything, the best way to deal with it is to name it. So Kant called them 'things-in-themselves'.

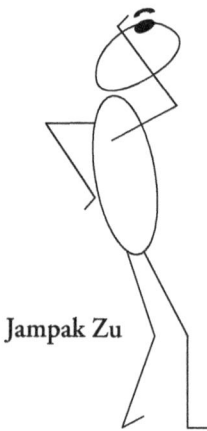

Jampak Zu

I wonder if **K** is writing this book to celebrate his ignorance about the physical world under the assertion that even Kant does not know. He looks like an incompetent school headmaster who speaks a lot with great courage without conviction, only to reveal to his students that he knows only as much as they know.

Thus, the cosmic structure of reality is a multi-layered one in almost one-to-one correspondence with the levels of human consciousness.

The reality has various levels or worlds starting from the ultimate reality of pure consciousness as shown in the Table 5.1.

Table 5.1 Level or World of Consciousness and Reality

Level / Degree / Form of Consciousness	Corresponding World / Level of Reality	Name in Theosophy
Pure Consciousness	World of pure consciousness (World of absolute reality or say absolutely real world)	*Adi lok*
(Available) God	World of (available) God or super soul(s)	*Anupadak lok*
Pure-I / *Atman* / Soul	World of souls	*Atman lok*
I-ness / *Aham* / Ego	World of egos	*Vijyanmay lok*
Mental Consciousness/Mind	Mental world (Reality of mental consciousness)	*Manomay lok*
Sense Consciousness	World of sense-consciousness	*Bhuvar lok*
Physical Objects (Zero Consciousness)	Physical world (Lowest form of reality)	*Bhu lok*

That reality has many levels is a very intriguing concept to me. There are two ways to look at this multiplicity of levels of reality or worlds. One is relativistic aspect and the other, holistic aspect. From the relativistic aspect, all the above seven worlds are nothing but different types of reality. In each world, objects of corresponding type of reality are phenomenally real while objects of other types of reality do not appear so. For example in the physical world, tables and chairs are phenomenally real and can be captured objectively while 'soul' is not a concrete, objectively accessible and scientifically (in natural science) verifiable reality. However, the latter must be real in its own world viz., world of souls or 'pure-I' where the physical objects such as table and chair may not be real.

From the holistic aspect, all the seven layers are not the types but degrees of reality, every higher world being more real than the lower one. In this way, pure consciousness is the absolute and only perfectly true reality and successively lower worlds are its diminishing manifestations or versions. It is only the light of pure consciousness that percolates all the way to the lower worlds to appear as consciousnesses of increasingly lesser intensity and higher limitations.

Thus, higher reality (or say higher consciousness) manifests itself in lower reality, which in turn manifests itself in still lower form. Hence, all the levels of reality fit into a cosmic scheme; a single picture where pure consciousness is the only absolute truth, only prime cause and rest all are successive effects of it. However, the lower levels of reality are not fully unreal. They are real to the extent they are the manifestations of absolute reality only.

This scheme of things is almost similar to the contention of Shankaracharya that in absolute terms or noumenally there is only one and single reality viz., pure consciousness and the physical world we live in, is *maya* or delusion which though phenomenally real, is ultimately unreal. It is only the pure consciousness that manifests itself as the world of objects.

Up to this point, our model about structure of reality is philosophical and metaphysical in nature. It may be said to be theosophical too, because of the close correspondence of our structure with theosophical line of thought. However, the inner flavour, approach and objective of my project are different. It will become visible as we proceed. This philosophical treatment of the subject has given us the frame of reference and direction wherein we shall now dare use our knowledge about the laws of physical world.

Physical level *(Bhu lok)*   This level of reality is manifested in the existence of material objects of physical world e.g., table, chair, human body, trees, earth etc.

Level of sense consciousness *(Bhuvar lok)*   It is manifested in the primal consciousness possessed by the senses.

Level of mental consciousness *(Manomay lok)*   This is represented by the consciousness that synthesizes the sense data, both intrinsic and extrinsic, understands and conceives it. It is the consciousness possessed by mind.

Level of consciousness of 'I-ness' or ego or *aham* **(***Vijyanmay lok***)**   This is the centre of person-hood. Kant calls it 'synthetic unity of apperception'. It roughly corresponds to ego or *aham*.

Level of consciousness of 'pure-I' or *atman* **(***Anandamay lok***)**   Since 'I-ness' is connected with person-predicates (body-mind), it ends with the physical death of person, while 'pure-I' or *atman* continues to exist and is beyond birth and death.

Level of (available) God or super-soul (*Anupadak lok***)**   It is the incomplete carbon copy or snapshot of pure consciousness cognizable by human mind.

Level of Pure Consciousness (*Adi lok***)**   This is the highest level of consciousness which is both the absolute truth and the ultimate knower. It is the ultimate source of all other levels of consciousness.

SIX

The Roadmap
...From Physics to 'Realics'

MY *PURPOSE* is to develop a cosmic physics…a physics that may be so general in flavour and coverage that it is applicable to all the layers of reality alike and not only to the physical reality. Just as physics deals with the physical reality, there may be a prospective science that dares to deal with all the realities, all its versions and its structure *in toto*. This may be called 'realics'…of course, if you like the word! Physics then shall be a special case of 'realics'.

We shall try to reach at realics, starting from physics. To reach at an *unknown general* from the *known special* is a historically verified path of evolution of knowledge. First was the development of Newtonian mechanics which dealt with the motions of moving objects that we see in our day-to-day life such as rocket, car and tennis ball. Relativistic mechanics of Einstein and successors, which dealt with the full range of motions (that is up to the speed of light… the maximum possible limit), was developed in the early decades of 20th Century, much after the development of Newtonian mechanics. It was found that Newtonian mechanics is capable of dealing only with slow moving objects with speeds much below that of light in free space. So it became just a special case of the relativistic mechanics. Similarly, the quantum relativistic mechanics that is even more general than the relativistic mechanics was developed much after the latter. In every development, physics grew more general rendering its own previous version a special case of the new found generality.

Here, I have discussed these examples to gain confidence and emulate this dialectics for moving from known and smaller realm of physics to unknown and larger region of realics. This shall be made possible by extending the laws of physics, to non-physical levels of reality, after some logical (or appearing logical!) modifications.

Firstly, I shall try to find a precise mathematical definition of this physical world. I shall then summarize the principal axioms and laws of physics applicable to this physical world. Next step will be to extract and list out those parameters from the axioms and laws which define this world or the level of physical reality. It will be these parameters which will act like knobs in the sense that by regulating or changing their values and meanings we will translate from physical world to any other world or level of reality. I shall then try to chalk out the pattern of variation of those parameters in any such inter-world translation. Once we conceive such a pattern logically, we can generalize axioms and laws of physics to develop them into cosmic science of all realities i.e., 'realics'. So let us focus on the very first step.

SEVEN

Physics
...All That We Think
We Know About This World

Generations were lost to know what we know
Now at a crossroad where to go;
Physics wedded maths and monkey became man
Wed spirituality to be God if you can.

*H*OW CAN this physical world we live in, which obeys laws of physics, be defined? This is not a simple question to answer. I am in need of a scientific definition. Can you define this world scientifically?... If we define it as a world of objects that can be captured by sense perception or the world of sensible objects, it lacks generic scientificity. This answer is psychological and philosophical in nature while we want a precise scientific-mathematical definition of the physical world. Besides it is a question begging definition as it refers to sense consciousness which itself is a non-physical reality. If we define it as world of object having zero consciousness, this definition is relatively precise but the problem of referring to consciousness remains. I have one precise and quantitative definition in mind:

"The physical world is one that encompasses all the objects having some speed(s) from zero to that of light in any frame of reference (x y z t)."

All the elementary particles from photon and neutrino to gigantic celestial bodies fall in this range. In any reference frame the minimum possible observable speed is zero and the maximum possible observable speed is that of light in free space, traditionally represented by 'c'. Nothing in this world can move faster than the speed of light in free space.

After defining it scientifically, now let us briefly revisit our basic understanding of the physical world which comes to us in the form of fundamental axioms and laws of physics that govern this world. You know, axioms are the basic ideas of something which we take as *a priori* truths to start with. They are different from laws as they remain unproved or unprovable, being the starting points of our thinking. For example, the idea of natural numbers, space and time, and matter and energy.

It took centuries to develop physics as it is today. In the history of physics, laws came, ruled and were defeated and replaced by the superior laws as the kings and the queens of history. The process is still on. You will be surprised to find that the laws which were derived or discovered starting with some axioms or *a priori* understandings went to change back those axioms themselves. They can be seen as the stances of rebellion amongst the community of ideas and laws in the history of physics! Anyway, let us dive into it...

The Space

There is a continuum or schema of free space wherein all physical objects and events find their place. Instantaneous positions and boundaries of objects can only be specified with respect to some reference-frame(s) in space. This free space is like bare infinite expansion. By default or by its very nature, it cannot have its own boundary. Had there been a boundary, that boundary could only be defined with respect to some reference-frame external to free space while all possible reference-frames that are thinkable shall be in the free space 'only'. Besides, if there is a boundary of free space, what can be outside the boundary other than free space? As we cannot answer this question, it is intellectually most comfortable to assume that there is a free space of infinite expansion...absolutely independent of anything else. This is the common sense account of space which, as you will see, suffered historic onslaught both by the developments of physics and philosophy.

The Time

There is a flux of time which represents a scale against which any change in the physical world is inherently felt and the rate of change is quantitatively measured by collective [human] consciousness. It is like a number counter that runs independently, indefinitely and infinitely, on which events or changes can be marked or represented in succession. If space is expansion, time is succession. This flux of time is due to the natural clock representing cosmic succession of events. It is felt from within and can be measured quantitatively by means, outside conscious self.

This is the common sense account of time. Newton put this classical and common sensical view of time in a scientific package when he wrote in his *Principia Mathematica* that 'absolute, true and mathematical time, of itself and from its own nature, flows equably without relation to anything external.' This description underlines two characters of time which are most fundamental to the classical view of time:

One, that the time is 'absolute'. It stands apart from anything else in nature. Its flow is self-consistent, self-contained and independent of everything else.

Two, the flow of time is 'equable'. This flow is one and the same for every point of the universe and for every sentient being. It is as if there is one universal clock for the entire universe or there are clocks at every point of universe and they are all synchronized. Hence, time beats in symphony throughout the [physical] world.

Thus, given the human consciousness, there is a time and space schema. We see everything spaced and timed. It is the way human consciousness is destined to perceive the physical world.

The Speed

All the particles/bodies in the physical world have some speed between zero to 'c'. Speed is defined as the rate of change of position i.e., change of position-in-space divided by time elapsed.

Speed = Change in position/corresponding change in time

Hence, speed is a derived quantity. As a concept, it comes only next to space and time, the latter two seem more fundamental, mathematically.

However physically, speed is as fundamental as space and time. You will see that in modern physics speed has emerged as the most important parameter which affects every other parameter in certain ways. In pages to come, you will find the speed altering our basic understanding of space and time.

There is another simple concept of 'relative speed'. It is the speed as perceived by some observer i.e., the speed relative to that observer. Suppose Tom is moving with a speed of 5 kmph in any direction and Jerry is following him with a speed of 3 kmph in the same direction. To Jerry, Tom will appear moving ahead by 5 – 3 = 2 kmph. However, if Jerry is following Tom by 7 kmph, Tom will appear coming towards Jerry by 7 – 5 = 2 kmph. So these are the speeds of Tom relative to Jerry. The same moving Tom or Jerry may have different speed relativity to other observers. This may be childlike for most of you; still I wanted to illustrate it as 'most of you' does not mean 'all of you'.

The Mass

Classically, mass is defined as 'quantity of substance or matter' in a physical body. What is this matter? What is this matter made of? How much we know about the matter?... We know that every body of matter is made up of smaller particles – atoms/subatomic particles. This book in front of you is made up of atoms of so many elements which in turn are made up of electrons, neutrons and protons. Protons and neutrons themselves are composed of quarks and so on. However, we do not know the real essence of mass.

A bigger body of mass is made up of smaller bodies which in turn are made up of even smaller bodies worthy to be called 'particles' and so on. But what is mass? What is its essence which gives it existential and coercive substantiality? What is the principle of its being? These questions explore the philosophical 'what' of mass is...which physics cannot answer. That a massive body is made up of smaller particles of mass (say proton or neutron) is no answer.

Even the most fundamental particle of mass we may know at any point of time will stand for the want of foundational meaning of mass. What mass is, we do not know. We do not know its physics; we do not know its philosophy. Our knowledge about mass is desperately limited. And even more shocking...we can measure it with precision. All our today's physics rests on this measurement with all the confidence of the world. It means not only that you do not know, but you also do not know that you do not know!

It is an emotional shock to **K**, it seems, that we can measure something without knowing its inner essence and existential meaning.... How can there be a mathematics of something in the absence of its philosophy?... So if you do not know something about anything, better do

Jampak Zu

not know anything about that thing...its intellectual fascism of philosophy against mathematics and physics or its cynical bowdlerizing of one knowledge for the other. It is all the big bad phrases applicable!

For the time being, let us settle with whatever we know and do not know. So all physical objects, all bodies of mass are at the bottom aggregate of subatomic particles of mass. In geometry, 'particle' is defined as having no dimension but only location. On the other hand, the physical particles of mass have dimensions and they cover space howsoever small it may be. However, the negligibility of their dimension makes them worthy of the word 'particle'.

The Energy

Classically, energy means capacity to do work. Energy is the principle of motion or potential of motion...the prime mover of any body or particle of mass. It has many forms, one convertible into another. Electromagnetic energy can be converted into thermal energy or heat; heat can be converted into light and sound etc. Work is also a form of energy. There are too many formulae and methods in physics to calculate and measure various forms of energy. For students of physics, all this is too obvious and known to be interesting. However, these premises of elementary physics have the potential to spin such childish looking but lethal questions which can crumble the hardest of faiths in our understanding of this world.

It is difficult to define energy. It has so many varied forms that one definition cannot cover. Like mass, we do not know the essence of energy as well. All attributes and formulae to calculate energy together cannot tell the 'philosophical what' of energy. What energy is made of? Energy makes tennis ball move, atoms bounce and vibrate, bombs explode, atoms emit quanta of light and so on. Once I asked a professor of physics, "What is there in the energy that enables it to do all this?" He smiled with sarcasm and told me that there is nothing in energy; rather it is energy which can do all this. Then his eyes told me that the he knows all about energy.... So, no further argument please. I rebelled and asked, "Sir, that energy can do this or that is the character or attribute of energy. But what is energy?" He got annoyed and said, "Nothing! It is just a name. Happy?" How could I be happy with such a rude answer. I wanted inside-out-type analysis of energy to get its objective existential validity and essential meaning...to be able to pin down that this is called 'energy'. Probably, the professor was right. It is just a name for something that we do not know intrinsically, completely and philosophically.

I think space, time, mass and energy—all the building blocks of physics are wrapped in the cloud of definitional and foundational vagueness. They all are like God! We know but we do not know. As we pray but we do not know fully...we calculate but we do not know fully.

The Relativity: Aristotle to Newton

This is probably the single most important topic in physics in terms of turbulences it has created in the common sensical world view made by most of us out of our day-to-day experiences. Relativity is the essence of all our perceptions, observations and measurements. We always define location of a particle in space relative to a reference frame. Likewise, we always define motion of the particle as change in its location relative to that reference frame. We cannot define location or motion of anything in barren, unqualified and unmarked space without any reference frame. If there is a particle of dust in a room, its location can be defined by its distance from all the three corners or walls of the room. Here, room and its corners act as a reference frame.

Basically, reference frame is a virtual mathematical construct of a relative perceptual standpoint. We can choose any reference frame with any set of three orthogonal (mutually perpendicular) axes with their point of intersection as origin of the frame to define location or motion of a particle or body in space. For example, a reference frame with three orthogonal axes—X, Y and Z is shown in Figure 7.1. Their intersection 'O' is the origin. Relative to this reference frame position of a point system 'P' is described as (x y z).

Different reference frames may give different coordinates of location or different account of motion for the same particle or body. For example, if a passenger drops a tennis ball in a moving train, his reference frame of perception is attached to the train and he will see the ball dropping straight down and bouncing up straight back. For another

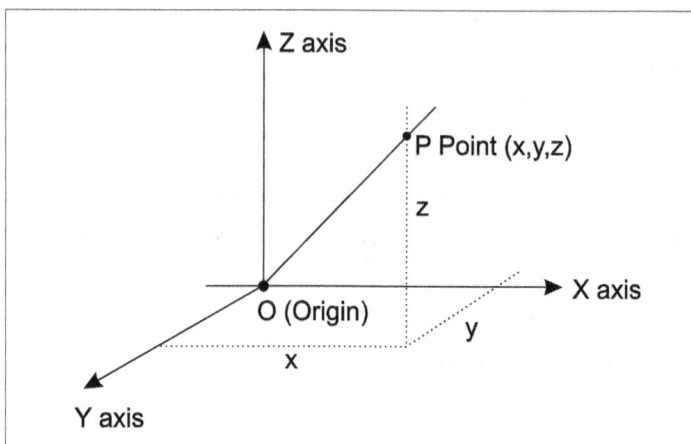

Fig. 7.1 Position of a point system 'P' observed in a reference frame (X Y Z)

observer say a gang-man standing by the side of rail line on the ground, the reference frame is attached to the earth. He will see ball dropping in parabolic motion and bouncing back up to hand of passenger parabolically. In the mean time, the positions of passenger and ball will become entirely different from initial ones with respect to earth. Hence, two different reference frames give two different perceptual viewpoint of same motion.

Whose viewpoint is more correct?... Today's physics says that both are equally correct. We cannot give any preference to any particular reference frame over the other. We may choose various other reference frames and each will give different measurements of location and motion of the ball. However, all such different observations are mathematically related according to the relative motion of

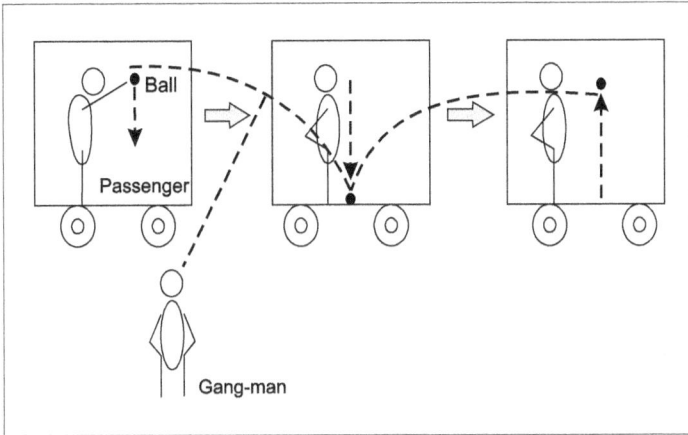

Fig. 7.2 Two different perceptual viewpoints of the same motion observed in two different reference frames

the reference frames with respect to each other. We can also choose a reference frame attached to the tennis ball itself. This particular reference frame will move with ball and will always find the ball at rest but everything else around such as earth, train and passenger moving. Its analogy is the earth itself which is like a moving ball around the sun. We standing on the earth (with reference frame attached to it) never directly observe its own motion. All this may seem too simple to the students of physics to waste time upon in reading but relativity throughout its evolution has caused historic intellectual indigestions to scientific-philosophical-religious world intelligentsia many a time.

In the early pages of history books (as early as 340 BC), there comes a great Greek philosopher **Aristotle** who had reasoned out that the natural and *ab initio* state of any physical body is 'rest' or motionlessness. It only 'comes' into motion on action of an impulse or force and later 'goes back' into its preferred state of rest. Bodies remain at rest 'by default' and move 'by force'. So rest is natural preference over motion. Hence, a reference frame of observation attached to a body at rest is the most perfect in defining a motion and hence must be preferred over a reference frame attached to a moving body.

Now a question arises—What is at rest and what is in motion? Aristotle again reasoned out that earth was perfectly stationary. Obviously, a reference frame attached to earth was absolutely perfect frame for observation. This conclusion was resting on the common sense observation that earth is the stationary foundation and all the moving bodies, be it train (say bullock cart for Aristotle), planet or stars move relative to the resting earth. Thus in the Greek account, our earth became the God's choice to be the perfectly stationary centre of universe and all celestial bodies were believed to be moving around the earth in perfectly circular orbits.

Around 140 AD, another great Greek philosopher **Ptolemy** developed a grand geocentric model of the universe. According to his model, Earth as the centre of cosmos was surrounded by eight mystical spheres carrying orbits of Moon, Mercury, Venus, Sun, Mars, Jupiter and fixed stars of sky respectively. For more than a millennium, Ptolemy's model remained the most accepted world view and all the astronomical observations used to be interpreted on its basis. It worked reasonably well for stars. However, the model was unable to fully explain the irregular motion of planets which seemed wandering in the background of fixed stars. Hence, they were called 'planets'. Word 'planet' follows from the Greek term *planeta* which means 'wanderer'. Motion of the moon was even more problematic to explain in this geocentric scheme.

Many attempts were made decades and centuries down the line to overcome these anomalies by introducing epicycles in Ptolemy's model. Epicycles are types of paths traversed when smaller circular orbits roll around a larger circular orbit. With the passage of time more refined astronomical data were gathered only to find new anomalies and mismatches in the model. In an effort to cope with new-found problems, epicycles went on becoming more complex. The old Ptolemic geocentric model was overloaded with complex modifications and patchworks of epicycles and oscillations. However, all efforts failed to explain the new irregularities found by further astronomical observations.

Perhaps, history was no longer ready to carry the errors committed by Aristotle and Ptolemy. In 16th Century, a Polish astronomer and clergyman, **Nicolas Copernicus** proposed a hypothesis dramatically opposite to the prevailing notion of geocentric universe. His hypothesis had two important points:

First, the earth was spinning on its own axis. Hence, the apparent motion of stars around the earth is caused by the relative motion of the observer standing on the spinning earth against the nearly fixed background of stars.

Second, the earth was neither stationary nor centre of the universe. If we assume sun at the centre, the anomalies in the movement of planets stand explained! They no longer remain 'wanderer'...and earth too becomes one among many planets around the sun rather than the divine choice of being the centre of universe.

This showed how relativity of motion could create illusions, strong enough to become part of our common sense world view. However out of fear of opposition from church, Copernicus kept his ideas to himself throughout, to be published as *On Revolution of Celestial Spheres* only with the end of his life. Church denounced the hypothesis and banned his book. However, death had already saved Copernicus from the wrath of the Vatican.

Men die but ideas never. The early decades of 17th Century witnessed one more rebel against church and the common sensical world view. He was the Italian scientist **Galileo Galilei**. With the help of his newly invented telescope, Galileo found Venus revolving around the sun and not the earth! He also saw small moons orbiting around Jupiter which implied that not all celestial bodies in the universe need to orbit around the earth. These findings were strong enough to kick the earth out of the centre of universe and endorse the hypothesis of Copernicus. Vatican summoned Galileo and ordered him to withdraw his findings. For about a decade, Galileo submitted to church but seeds of intellectual upheaval were already sown. Fortunately, both history and Platonic ideas are not like computers where you can undo any event with a click of a mouse. Vatican forgot that the mouse of universe and human history was only with the God, if you believe He is, and not with any religious institution in the world. In 1632, Galileo courageously published his firework titled *Dialogue* endorsing Copernican hypothesis at the cost of widespread humiliation and life imprisonment.

Almost at the same time, another German astronomer **Johannes Kepler** with the help of huge amount of astronomical data showed that planets move in elliptical orbits rather than circular ones. Kepler's modification perfected the evolving picture of universe in which the astronomical data were now matching perfectly with it. Now we had the idea of heliocentric planet system with the sun at the centre and the planets revolving in elliptical orbits with the background of fixed stars.

Keplar's hypothesis was based on mere observations. He was still unable to explain why the planets revolve in elliptical orbits around sun. The explanation came after about seven decades when the English mathematician and physicist **Sir Isaac Newton** published his *Philosophiae Naturalis Principia Mathematica* in 1687. Therein he proposed his famous law of universal gravitation which says that every body of mass attracts every other body and the gravitational attraction between the two bodies depends on their mass and distance between them. This gravitational force explains not only the fall of an object on the earth but also the elliptical motion of planets around the sun. This was the final blow to the age-old world view of Aristotle and Ptolemy.

In *Principia Mathematica,* Newton also developed complete physics and mathematics of motion of bodies. Newtonian physics fostered a new world view entirely different from the ancient Greek one. It can be summarized in following set of ideas:

a. Universe is infinite with infinite number of celestial bodies spread throughout this infinitude.
b. Every celestial [and non-celestial] body is attracting every other body by gravity. So every body of mass, be it a tennis ball, the earth, the sun or the stars is under the effect of [gravitational] force by all other bodies.
c. For a body to move with a uniform velocity no force is required. Force is required only to accelerate a body. Hence, the Aristotelian notion that the preferred or natural state of a body is 'rest' and it moves only when a force or impulse is applied was not found. There is no such thing like preferred or natural state of rest.
d. Following the idea of relativity developed by Galileo, Newton found that if a body A is moving with respect to body B (i.e., for an observer fixed with B), mathematically it is equally good to say that body B is moving with respect to A in opposite direction.

It logically follows from the above notion of relativity that we cannot define who is absolutely at rest and who is moving. All the motion and rest of bodies are definable only relative to each other...and the absence of absolute rest means, there is no absolute reference frame against which we can measure and define location of other points of space. Hence, all the positions of objects and events and distances between them are relative. All the accounts of space is relative. Different observers will find different accounts of locations and distances of objects and events. Interestingly, all will be true.

This is what logically comes out of Newton's physics. Though Newton's mind was so much trained in the traditional common sensical views of 'absolute space' and 'absolute rest' in vogue through generations that he was unable to accept the logical outcome of his own theory. However, Newton's theory was more powerful than him and he could not stop the evolution of his own ideas.

I think an idea has its own élan vital, own life and own potential. It does not depend on the potential of the thinking mind. If a mind is unable to carry its own idea, it may switch to another mind. Probably, Plato was right in claiming that ideas have independent existence.

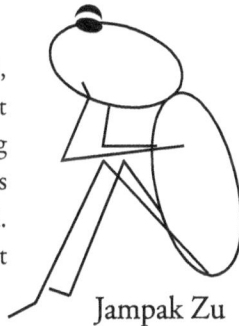

Jampak Zu

As per the laws of motion [Point (c) mentioned before] formulated by Newton, a system in absence of any external force on itself moves only with constant velocity. Such systems (or reference frames associated with such systems) are called 'inertial systems' (or inertial reference frames). Inertial systems have no acceleration i.e., no change of speed or direction. Newton had assumed that a reference frame fixed with respect to distant stars is an inertial system. Usually, we take earth too as an inertial system neglecting all the small acceleration due to its spinning or orbital motion or the motion of whole solar system. This is just an approximation for the ease of calculations. Thus, any reference frame attached to earth or at uniform velocity with respect to earth, e.g., a car moving with constant speed in same direction, becomes an inertial reference frame too.

(However, there is no need to refer to distant stars for defining an inertial reference frame. Newton did so as he was not comfortable with the idea of absence of absolute space and absolute rest. For him, the distant stars constituted fixed reference of absolute rest which is not true. You will see in the coming pages that in the early 20th Century, Einstein provided for the perfect understanding of inertia reference frames.)

There was one thing not yet captured by the growing understanding of human mind about the nature of nature. It was 'time'. Newton simply followed the ancient Greek notion of time as absolutely independent and universal flux manifested in succession of events. This was the common sense and simplistic view of time. Newtonian physics was not competent enough to discover the real and definitional essence of time in all its relatedness with the other aspects of nature. Hence, it was satisfied and settled with the traditional vagueness of understanding of time.

However, a breakthrough in the understanding of time came from the great German philosopher **Immanuel Kant**. He analysed the process of cognition and conception in great depth and revealed that time [together with space] are 'pure percepts'. They are intrinsic elements of every perception. Our mind is programmed to see objects and events spaced and timed. Hence, as pure and essential elements of every perception they follow from mind. Our mind cannot see any object or event unspaced and untimed...i.e., stripped of space and time. So time and space are limiting rules of perception given by the mind. Existence of space and time independent of mind is not found, undiscoverable and inexplicable. Whether time and space exist independently is a pseudo question as we do not know what we are asking...we have never seen time or space independent of our mind.... Yeah, that is a good dose of philosophy!

God created nature to amuse and confuse the man. Man created philosophy to help God in doing so.

Jampak Zu

For those not trained in philosophy, it may be a bit difficult to understand and appreciate Kant but he did two great things. One, he bracketed time and space in one category. Two, he refuted the reality of independent and absolute time. You will see that the womb of time had another great personality to do the same two things on a scientific ground.

The Relativity: New Light of Einstein

There was another thing which was not yet captured by the Newtonian age physics and that was light. Light was never thought to be an important player in the game of physics. Light reciprocated in the same fashion and hence there was darkness in the understanding of relativity!

In 1864, an English physicist **James Clerk Maxwell** found that electricity and magnetism are not independent but related fields. Electricity can produce magnetism and magnetism can produce electricity. He unified the two into one complete theory of electromagnetism and wrote generalized equations for electromagnetic fields. These are known as 'Maxwell equations'. Maxwell equations predicted that under certain conditions there may appear disturbances of electromagnetic fields which can travel in space in wave forms at certain speed. They were called 'electromagnetic waves'. From Maxwell equations their speed in free space or vacuum was calculated to be about 300,000 km per second. That was also the speed of light as found experimentally! Electromagnetic waves were also predicted to have other properties like dispersion and polarization…all of which were found properties of light as well. Hence, light was proved to be an electromagnetic wave following Maxwell equations and travelling at fixed speed in space.

This development seems simple but was actually the biggest challenge to the concept of relativity. We have seen that it logically follows from Newtonian physics that there is no absolute space or absolute rest. The location and motion of all objects and the location of all events can at best be measured relative to some reference frame. One reference frame itself may move relative to other reference frame and then they will give different accounts of similar motion of same object. (As we saw that the passenger in train gives different account of the motion of tennis ball dropping in train from a gang-man standing near the rail line in Figure 7.2)

Now if Maxwell's theory predicts that speed of light in free space is fixed, it is fixed relative to what? I mean relative to which reference frame? There could be two possibilities: Either there is some universal and absolute reference to which it is fixed or it is fixed relative to all possible inertial reference frames.

First possibility was the natural choice as common sense notion of relativity had ruled out the second possibility.

To say that the speed of light is same in all possible inertial reference frames is unthinkable. Different inertial reference frames may move constantly but with different speeds in different directions with respect to each other. How can then the speed of light be same in all such reference frames? Our common sense notion of relativity says that if Tom is moving with speed of 60 km per hour and Jerry is following Tom with speed of 30 km per hour, Jerry will see

Tom moving ahead of him only at 60 – 30 = 30 km per hour. Now replace Tom with a ray of light travelling with the speed of light 'c' and choose a reference frame, say an imaginary jet plane, in place of Jerry following the ray of light with half the speed viz., c/2. According to common sense relativity, the pilot of jet plane should see the light travelling with speed c – c/2 = c/2. Thus, common sense dictates that pilot of the jet that forms an inertial reference frame will not find the speed of light in free space as 'c'.

Hence, only the first possibility is left. It was assumed for long that all the space including free space is filled universally and uniformly with an invisible substance named 'ether' which acts as the medium through which the light travels. So the speed of light was assumed to be fixed relative to ether. This hypothetical ether was providing the universal reference frame to satisfy the hangover of absolute space and absolute reference frame at rest.

However, we have seen that the logical outcome of Newtonian physics was the absence of any universal or absolute reference frame. (It is a different matter that Newton believed in absolute space and ether to be absolute reference frame.) So if the first possibility is at variance with the spin-off ideas of Newtonian physics and the second possibility is unthinkable as per common sense notion of relativity, nothing remains to go with?

The intellectual mess created by the historical forces was cleared when in 1887 **Albert A Michelson** and **Edward Morley** revealed experimentally that there is no such thing like ether. Had there been a universal reference frame of ether, the speed of light would have been fixed relative to that but not relative to other reference frames or other observers. Michelson and Morley claimed that if earth is moving through ether, the speed of light parallel and perpendicular to the motion of earth must be observed differently. They measured the speed of light in both the directions with great accuracy and it came out to be the same! So ether was not found.

Michelson and Morley experiment established what was flowing logically from Newton viz., there is no universal reference frame, no absolute space, no absolute rest and motion. All the kinematics (rest and motion) is relative to specific frames or observers and all the relative observations and measurements are correct in their own place. None is more accurate or correct than the other.

Now again the original problem appeared. If the speed of light as calculated by Maxwell's equations is fixed in the free space, it is fixed relative to what?…Was the second possibility the answer? Is the speed of light 'c' fixed relative to all possible inertial reference frames? If so, it would mean that for an observer chasing light with a speed which is almost equal to 'c' (say 1 km per second less than 'c') light will still appear to be moving away from him at speed of 'c' only.… Common sensically, it seems unthinkable.

Now came the greatest hero on stage in the historic drama of physics. A failure in his college examinations…a model dropout…rejected from various jobs of teaching…a petty clerk in the Swiss patent office of Berne. CHARACTER'S NAME: **Albert Einstein**; AGE: 26 years.

In 1905, Einstein published three papers. One of these was his 'theory of special relativity'. (The other two were on the quantum character of light and Brownian motion.) Einstein proposed two postulates:

1. The laws of physics are same in all inertial reference frames. So there is no preferred or absolute inertial reference frame. (All the inertial reference frames move at constant velocity relative to each other).

2. Speed of light in free space is same relative to all inertial reference frames.

These two simple looking and elegant postulates revolutionized all our understanding of space, time, motion, rest, mass, energy and so on. Consequent upon these postulates were some remarkable conclusions. Let us go through some of them one by one.

Relativity of Time and Time Dilation

Einstein found that it is possible to have same speed of light in all inertial reference frames if we are ready to shun the age-old notion of absolute and independent time. He showed that to an observer a moving clock would tick slowly than a resting clock. This phenomenon is termed as 'time dilation' in the books of physics. As we experience only very slow speeds compared to the speed of light, we never find the difference in our day-to-day life. However, it becomes prominent when speed [of clock] becomes comparable to the speed of light. Moreover, higher the speed of clock, slower becomes the ticking rate of clock. Surprisingly, this dependence of rate of ticking of clock on its observed speed applies not only on manmade clocks but also on all the processes of nature, be it physical, chemical, biological or any other. In fact, this effect of speed on the flux of time has been experimentally verified on muons (a type of subatomic particles) and in other ways too.

When high-energy particles of cosmic rays from upper space reach the earth's atmosphere, they create a type of subatomic particles called 'muons'. These muons immediately and automatically decay or disintegrate into electrons. Three facts that may be noted are:

Fact no.1   On an average a 'resting' muon decays into electron in 2×10^{-6} seconds i.e., within 0.000002 second or around one millionth part of a second.

Fact no.2   As muon is created, it starts moving towards the earth with the speed of about 0.998c (2.994×10^8 metres per second) i.e., nearing the speed of light.

Fact no.3   After its creation in the upper atmosphere, it travels about 6,000 metres down to the earth's surface.

Now if the life of muon is only 0.000002 second, it can move in its life span by $0.000002 \times 2.994 \times 10^8$ metres per second that comes about 600 metres only! Then how a muon travels over 6,000 metres and reaches successfully to the earth's surface?

Relativity is the answer. Muon's life span is 0.000002 second only when it is resting. However for an observer standing on the earth, muon is moving at a high speed of 0.998c. So for this observer the time of muon will beat slower. (However, muon will see its life as 0.000002 second only because for an observer attached to muon itself, muon will always be at rest.) With slower beat of time, its life span will increase accordingly and it will travel over 6,000 metres and reach the earth's surface before decaying. It is astonishing if you feel deeply that the life clock of a moving muon ticks slowly for the observer on the earth though it decays within 0.000002 second in its own reference frame.

Einstein's special relativity predicts another similar phenomenon. Suppose A and B are twins. A lives on the earth as we do and B is settled in a space shuttle of extremely high speed. Further suppose B continues to travel at extremely high speed till A becomes very old. When B would return back to earth to meet A, A will find B younger than himself e.g., A will be 45-year-old while B may be just 30-year-old…despite the fact that they took birth together. This happens because under high speed the natural (biological and mental) clock of B goes slower than that of A and hence the ageing rate of B is lesser than that of A. This phenomenon is known as 'twin paradox'.

All this shows that the beat of time or natural rate of succession of events [of physical reality] is not a universal and absolute proposition. It depends on the speed of observed relative to observer. Therefore, time is a relative concept. There is no time independent of observation. Our common sense was shown to be wrong by physics! It happened probably because our world views and common sense grow out of our experience and in our daily life we never experience reference frames (or observers) having speed near to that of light. So our common sense notion of relativity remains incomplete for want of high speed experiences. Einstein turned our basic understanding of nature, especially of 'time' topsy-turvy.

Giving philosophical tongue to Einstein's relativity we can say that time is in the mind and not outside it. We have seen that Immanuel Kant too speaks of similar intentions. It is incidental that both the heroes of physics and philosophy hailed from Germany and they reached at the same point, though through different courses.

Relativity of Space and Length Contraction

It follows from the relativity that any measurement of distance between two points or length of an object is different for different observers and depends on the relative motion of the two points or the object under observation and the observer. Einstein showed that to an observer any distance or length gets shorter when there is such relative motion. It means for an observer a measuring scale will become shorter when it moves along the length. This phenomenon is called 'length contraction' or 'Lorentz-FitzGerald contraction' in the textbooks of physics.

Let us revisit the previous example of travelling of muons from upper sky to the earth's surface from a different perspective viz., that of space or distance instead of time. How does a muon with small life span of 0.000002 second travel a distance of 6,000 metres? Actually, it is only the observer attached to earth (like us) who sees that muon is travelling the distance of 6,000 metres from sky to the earth. Since muon is moving with high speed of 0.998c, the distance between upper sky from where it started its journey and the surface of earth which is 6,000 metres for us will contract to 600 metres for muon. So a muon (or a virtual observer attached to it) will see itself covering only 600 metres before touching the earth's surface.

Thus, to a moving observer (like muon) the distance covered gets shortened. Similarly, to an observer the length of a moving object gets shortened. Both are the same phenomena, relativistically, as in the former case, the observer moves against an observed coverable distance/ length and in the latter, the observed length [of object] moves against the observer. All we need is a relative motion of observer and observed distance/length and the latter gets shortened.

So any distance/length which is just a dimension of a piece of space is dependent on the relative speed of observer and observed. Since no motion and rest is absolute, we can never claim that the distance between any two points is only this. Different observers will measure the same distance differently and all will be true from their standpoint.

Actually before Einstein, Lorentz had proposed the equations which calculate how much time dilation or length contraction will take place at what relative speed of observer and observed. However, Lorentz had used the earlier notion of universal reference frame of ether. Einstein used the same equations for his special relativity but gave different interpretation of it obviating the need of ether. These equations, named by **Poincare** after Lorentz, are popularly known as 'Lorentz transformation equations'.

One-ness of space and time

Let us move further. Suppose a wave of light is sent from one place to another. Any observer in its reference frame can observe three parameters:

1. T, the time taken by wave of light to travel from one place to another
2. D, the distance travelled by flash of light in that time i.e., distance between the two places
3. C, the speed of light which is distance travelled divided by time taken (C = D/T)

Suppose there are different observers each moving at constant speed (or resting) relative to one another. Newton would say that these different observers should find the relative speed of light, C different from each other but should agree that the time taken, T is same (as for Newton, time is universal and independent). Hence the distance, D (= CT) between the places should essentially be observed differently by different observers.

However as per the postulate of special relativity, the speed of light C is fixed. Hence, the different observers will find different values of the time taken (T) and the distance between the two places (D). These varied observations of time and distance will depend on the speed of reference frames relative to the places of events...and all the observations of time and distance will be equally true. What does this mean?... Tom may say that D is 3 metres and T is 2 seconds and Jerry will claim that the same D is 2 metres and T is 3 seconds. And both will be relatively true.

So our measuring tapes and clocks are intermixed! Some portion of the measuring tape of Tom is being measured by the clock of Jerry and vice versa. So what can be measured by tape can also be measured by clock and vice versa. It means distance (or space) and time are not different entities. They are the manifestations of one and the same entity. Physics did not want to give a new name for that. So we call it 'space-time'.

Henceforth, space by itself and time by itself,
are doomed to fade away into mere shadows,
and only a kind of union of the two
will preserve an independent reality.

Herman Minkowski

One-ness of mass and energy

Another astonishing outcome of the special theory of relativity was relativity of mass of a body. It means two observers moving with different velocities will see the same body as having different mass. As the relative speed of a body goes high, the perceived mass of the body also shoots up. Suppose there is a jet which can move at a very high speed of the order of light. A bar of 1 kg is put in the jet and the latter starts its flight. Pilot observes the bar at rest, so he perceives its 'rest mass' of 1 kg. The man at earth observes the jet, hence the bar moving at very high speed. So he may find its mass to be say 2 kg, 3 kg, 4 kg…depending on the speed of the jet.

The above example shows that a body with high speed and hence high kinetic energy also possesses high mass. In fact, whenever any body is injected with additional energy of any type, mass of the body increases. It means the mass and energy are equivalent. Mass can be taken as a form of energy…a type of compact, concrete energy…energy which can be weighed! So mass and energy are different manifestations of inherently the same thing. Rather than giving a new name to that inner thing, Physics calls it 'mass-energy'.

Einstein's most celebrated equation of $E = mc^2$ shows this very equivalence of mass and energy. It means the bar of 1 kg rest mass is equivalent to 1 kg $\times c^2$ energy. This equation is experimentally verifiable. In the process of nuclear fission or fusion, the total mass of reacting particles reduces and energy of equivalent amount following $E = mc^2$ is released. However, it is wrong to say that mass is destroyed and an equivalent amount of energy is released. In fact, the released energy also has mass which is equal to the missing mass in the fission or fusion reaction. So it is more correct to say that in such nuclear reactions the form of energy changes...from rest-mass energy to other usual and more familiar forms such as heat, sound, light and kinetic energy.

$E = mc^2$ is one of the greatest, mightiest and costliest equation in the history of Physics. The atomic and nuclear bombs follow this. Its greatness lies in its conceptual miracle. Its might we have seen during the World War II in Japan. It may cost us dear!

Wave–Particle: Quantum Nature of Light

The on going drama of physics had lots more to show to its audience. Do you know what is meant by a wave and what is a particle? Common sensically and conventionally, particle means a small point-like entity having concreteness, lumpiness, definite boundaries, potential solidity etc. Examples may be particle of dust or sand. On the other hand, wave means patterned disturbance which is distributed or spreads over a length or space, and is not lumped and moves as ripples. Examples are ripple waves on surface of water or sound waves in air.

There are certain properties which were conventionally considered to be possessed by particles only. For example, particles can hit and impact other particles. An electron can hit another stable electron and make the latter move. 'Pure waves' are not supposed to do so. If Tom has to throw 10 pure particles on Jerry in continuation, he can only throw them in discrete fashion, that is one by one.

However, if Jerry has to send 10 ripples of pure waves to Tom he can send them in continuous unbroken chain of waves. So conventionally, particles are supposed to travel as lumped and discrete packets…like postal packets of a courier service! On the other hand conventionally, pure waves are supposed to travel as unbroken, continuous flux of ripples…like non-stop flowing water in pipeline!

A new story starts now. CHARACTER'S NAME: **Max Planck**; AGE: 42 years; PLACE: University of Berlin; TIME: 1900; HOBBIES: Playing music, mountaineering; PASSION: Physics. Planck found that electromagnetic radiations emitted from a blackbody can be explained only if we assume that waves of radiation are emitted and absorbed in discrete steps. That means the electromagnetic waves in emission and absorption somehow behave as lumped packets of energy. So we can rightly think that in a beam of light there exist many discrete packets or bursts or 'particles of energy'. This finding was completely at variance with the conventional understanding of wave nature and of light as electromagnetic wave in particular.

It was almost the same time when a new phenomenon was discovered. When you throw a beam of light on a metal plate it emits electrons in certain conditions. This is called 'photoelectric effect'. What puzzled the scientific community were the two features of this effect:

a. The energy of emitted electrons (called 'photoelectrons') was found to be dependent on the frequency of incident beam of light and not on its intensity. If light is purely a wave, energy of the photoelectron should have been proportional to the intensity of light.

b. There was no time lag in the arrival of light on metal surface and emission of photoelectrons. If light is a wave, its energy will be distributed and cannot be instantly transferred to an electron in metal to enable it to emit. It was as if light is made up of particles of energy that hit the electrons in metal to emit them out.

It was impossible to explain photoelectric effect assuming light as electromagnetic wave. Hero came again. Einstein in 1905 in his another paper on quantum nature of light proposed that photoelectric effect can be explained using hypothesis of Planck. He further showed that light is not only emitted and absorbed as packets or particles of energy but also propagates in that form. So a ray of light is basically a bunch of discrete packets of energy. These packets are called 'quanta' (singular: quantum). They are also called 'photons'. Photon means particle of light.

Max Planck had already given the equation that how much energy will be there in one quantum or photon.

This equation, famous as 'Planck's equation' is:

$$E = h\nu$$

('ν' is a Greek letter pronounced as *neu*.)

Here 'E' is the energy of a photon (particle of light), 'ν' is the frequency of photon and 'h' is called 'Planck's constant' whose value is 6.023×10^{-34} Joule second.

(I have avoided writing equations of physics in this book but this one is necessary as it will be used to find God! I thought Jampak Zu will say something sarcastic. He did not!)

Wave theory of light was well established much before Einstein and Planck as it was the only theory that could explain many optical effects like interference and diffraction. Hence, the fact that light is a wave was established is beyond doubt. Now quantum theory of light, after successfully explaining the photoelectric effect, established that light exhibits particle character too. It means light behaves as wave in certain observations and as particle in certain other observations. It has dual character.

The Particle...That is Wave

Likewise, there are certain properties which are conventionally considered to be possessed by waves only and not by particles. For example, the effect like interference and diffraction are supposed to be exibited by waves only because they can only be explained by wave theory. When a wave is passed through a small hole or a mesh or a grid it gets diffracted according to some pattern. When you throw torchlight on a magnifying glass, the light makes a definite pattern of beautiful rings on the wall at the other side of the glass. This is diffraction pattern. A conventionally pure particle is not considered to have this property.

Two decades elapsed after the discovery of particle properties of waves in 1905 when in 1924 another actor came on the stage of physics to suggest 'wave properties of particles'. CHARACTER'S NAME: **Louis de Broglie; AGE: 32; ACTIVITY:** Student of history…later physics. De Broglie suggested that every moving body in certain ways exhibits character of waves! This hypothesis is very simple and general in nature. It applies to all bodies and particles…be it a moving rocket, bullet shot, high speed electron or photon.

This was complimentary to what was expounded by Einstein and Planck viz., 'particle properties of waves'. Planck and Einstein had to fight a lot against the predominent views of their age despite having strong experimental evidences in their arsenal.

However, later the scientific community became so open-minded that hypothesis of de Broglie was given receptive attention even in absence of strong experimental support. Anyway, he did not have to wait for such supports for long. Within two years another big star of this drama **Erwin Schrödinger** developed what we call 'wave mechanics' and explained many intricate atomic phenomena using de Broglie's hypothesis.

However, direct support to de Broglie came from a great historic experiment done by **Davisson** and **Germer** in the United States in 1927. Davisson and Germer were studying the scattering pattern of electrons from a solid. In their lab apparatus, a pencil beam of electrons was made to strike a solid target. This solid target was a block of nickel. Vacuum was created in the apparatus to prevent oxidization of nickel block. However, something went wrong with the apparatus during experiment and air entered inside leading to oxidization of the nickel block. They removed the block and baked it on a high temperature oven to deoxidize it. The purified nickel block was put back in the apparatus and the experiment was restarted. Results were altogether different and surprising. The beam of electron after falling on the nickel block was being diffracted by the regular atomic arrays of nickel crystal.

Had the classical Newtonian physics been true, the electrons would have been scattered by the nickel block in all directions with continuous variation of scattered electron intensity with angle. Instead there were maxima and minima in the intensity of scattered electrons. This was the sign of diffraction…the property of wave! So electrons moving in beam were proved to be having wave properties.

You know, the baking of nickel block made all the difference. Actually, in a simple bar of nickel there are many small crystals made of regular three dimensional array of atoms. However, the bar as a whole remains irregular at atomic level as these small crystals are randomly joined in it. Baking at high temperature caused small crystals of nickel to form a single large crystal. In this way, the whole block of nickel became a big crystal with regular atomic arrays. These arrays worked as atomic grid or mesh on which waves of electrons fell to be diffracted.

Thus, a new history was written in experimental physics by accident in apparatus of Davisson and Germer. It was now established beyond doubt that a moving particle or body in certain observations exhibits wave properties also.

Many of the great or seemingly great things that happen in the history are by accidents. I doubt but if **K** becomes successful in impressing his hypothesis of nature on your mind...it will also be an accident. It will be like entering the vague and poetic air of consciousness into the apparatus of physics, accidentally to oxidize a scientific mind which was supposed to have vacuum of mathematical clarity. This book may be accident prone. So better stop reading ahead.

Jampak Zu

So all waves are particles too and every particle is also a wave. This we call 'wave-particle duality'. The two hitherto mutually exclusive propositions of 'particle' and 'wave' converged to render everything in this world, a dual character. This duality is more prominent, visible and experimentally verifiable when the moving system is very small and its speed is very high e.g., in case of light and fast moving subatomic particles.

It is notable that Einstein had suggested only dual character of light. De Broglie extended it to all the objects of physical reality. The 20th Century physics had entered into a realm of synthesis...that of time and space, mass and energy, wave and particle.

The Uncertainty and Matter Waves

First half of 20th Century was very eventful for physics. Galaxy of stars, rich stories, host of discoveries and non-stop drama, non-stop fun! History was favouring physics. So came another star on the stage. CHARACTER NAME: **Werner Heisenberg**; AGE: 26 years; NATIONALITY: German; HOBBIES: Mountaineering and skiing. In 1927, Heisenberg discovered the principle of uncertainty according to which there is some essential elemental uncertainty inherent in the physical world. This uncertainty pertains to the actual values of physical quantities like position, momentum, energy, time, etc. This uncertainty is in the very structure of physical reality; it has nothing to do with the precision or exactness of measuring equipment. No amount of care and precision on the part of measurement can remove this uncertainty, because the quantities of this physical world themselves are intrinsically, though very slightly, uncertain in value.

This is a very intriguing subject. Let us understand clearly and carefully what uncertainty means and how it is the integral character of everything that exists. By now we know that all the objects or systems of nature possess wave-particle duality. Every moving system of matter say a rocket or bullet or electron is physically and mathematically definable in terms of a set or package of some waves. These waves are called 'matter waves' or 'de Broglie waves'. It is an umbrella term which encompasses even electromagnetic wave of light associated with a moving photon.

So when a system is moving, we can safely say that some set of matter wave is associated with that system. An example has been illustrated graphically in Fig. 7.3. Here, a moving particle (more precisely a small spherical body say electron) is identified with a moving wave system. It is just for illustration.

We see that a simple body is represented by a complex structure of waves which is spread along the axis of motion. These matter waves basically exhibit the "probability of

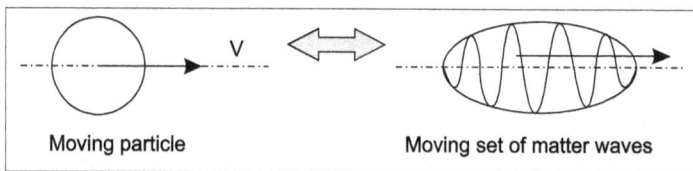

Moving particle   Moving set of matter waves

Fig. 7.3   Identification of a moving particle (say electron)
with a moving wave system

finding particle/matter" in space. So wherever the wave is high on the axis of motion, there will be higher probability of finding the particle or matter. In wave mechanics, the amplitude of matter wave at any point is called 'wave function' which is denoted by symbol 'Ψ' (the Greek letter 'psi', pronounced as 'sai'). A scientist **Max Born** had first shown that the probability of finding the particle/matter at any point in space is actually proportional to $|\Psi|^2$.

Let us consider Fig 7.4. Here, the circle represents a spherical body (say a solid ball) which is moving with speed

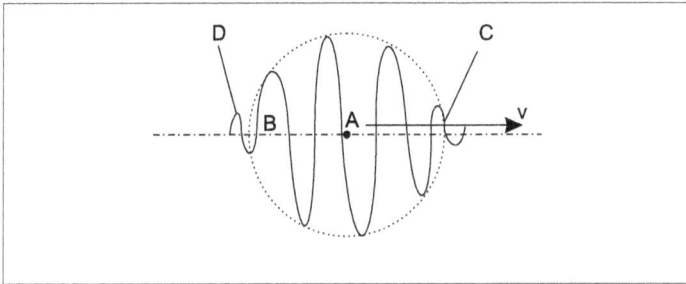

Fig. 7.4 Undefined boundary of a moving body due to matter waves associated with it

'v' along the axis of motion as shown. 'A' is the centre of the ball. The wave function is quite high at points A and B which are inside the moving system/body. That is because here the probability of finding matter is very high. We will surely find the matter of ball inside the ball. However, you will be surprised that students of wave mechanics always talk in terms of probability. What may be 100 per cent certain for a layman will be only 99.99…per cent probable for them. At point C, which is at the boundary of the system (surface of the ball), wave function is low…and surprisingly there is some (though very little) wave function even outside the boundary of the system at point D.

What does all this point to? It means to what we understand as boundary or surface of a physical body or system is not as precise, fine and definite as we think it to be in our day-to-day perceptions. A layman thinks that from point A up to C, there 'is' matter i.e., the probability of finding matter is 100 per cent and just after C i.e., just after the perceived surface, there is no matter belonging to that system and hence there should be zero probability of finding matter. However, wave mechanics tells a different story. There is actually some spreading of the system definition with a pattern of matter wave distribution that only 'almost' follows the system and with boundaries that are a bit vague and uncertain! That is why we are not fully sure of finding matter at and beneath the conventional surface of ball and on the other hand, there is some probability that we may find matter of the ball even outside this conventional surface.

The universal duality of wave and particle nature of any system renders the moving boundaries of the system 'less-than-precise' or 'less-than-fully definite'. Wave-ness of a matter system gives it some kind of fluidity or spread-ness. Thus, there is some structural uncertainty in the nature regarding the exact position of a system as its location is definable only in terms of the location of its boundaries.

Similarly, there are uncertainties in time, momentum, energy, etc., of a moving system. All uncertainties of various parameters are interconnected due to their common cause.

According to Heisenberg's theory of uncertainty, if 'x' is the position of a particle and 'p' is its momentum; and if 'Δx' is the natural uncertainty in position and 'Δp' is the uncertainty in momentum of the particle then their product or 'uncertainty product' (as I call it) is:

$$\Delta x \Delta p \approx h/2\pi$$

(Symbol 'Δ', pronounced as *delta*, is used to represent the uncertainty of value of any physical parameter and mathematical constant 'π' spelled out as *pi* is defined as the ratio of a circle's circumference to its diameter.)

Similarly, $\Delta E \Delta t \approx h/2\pi$

(Here, ΔE and Δt are natural uncertainties of energy and time respectively.)

Here 'h' is Planck's constant. Its value is very small; 6.023×10^{-34} Joule second. Hence, the structural uncertainty of the physical world is directly connected with the Planck's constant. It follows from the above equations that uncertainty-in-general found in nature, be it of any physical quantity viz., position, momentum, energy or time is proportional to the Planck's constant.

Courtesy the smallness of the Planck's constant 'h', the uncertainties in the physical world are very small and our physical world is 'almost certain'...it is certain enough to live a normal life. We in our day-to-day life never experience physical uncertainty. In this physical world, I know here is my table and chair; here is the physical body of my friend etc., with definite positions and boundaries. I know this is the speed of my car. I recognize with certitude the changing position of an aeroplane in the sky or a flying bee in my kitchen garden and so on. Our normal life in the physical world rests on our confidence in the precision and correctness of our perception. We know that things actually exist as we see them; they are actually where we see them and we can catch them where we see them existing. As laymen, we never find that there is any uncertainty in this world which interferes with our perception.

It is only at the subatomic level that uncertainty plays some meaningful role because systems (the subatomic particles and photons: the particles of light) are so small that any uncertainty in them turns out to be a considerable percentage of their actual size. Had the value of Planck's constant 'h' been considerably high, the way and import of life in the world we live might have been be entirely different. Imagine a case where uncertainty of the physical world would have been very high.

I would never have been sure of the positions of the various keys/buttons on my keyboard with which I am typing this book. The key of 'S' would then be spread over the neighbouring keys of 'Q', 'W', 'E', 'D', 'X', 'Z' and 'A'...probably even beyond that. The tip of my pen would not be pointedly defined. When I would start writing, there would have been a considerable area on the paper over which the tip of my pen could touch anywhere randomly! We might not have been able to insert a key in the socket of its lock that easily with repeated success...because the area of the socket and the area of the head of the key would not have been defined with required precision.

All the developments of modern science from space technology to nano-technology would not have been possible then. Indeed, the life would have been entirely different and difficult. We must be thankful to God that the value of Planck's constant 'h' is extremely small in the physical world.

I had never thought that to be thankful
to God I would have to be so technical!

Jampak Zu

Now revisit the Planck's equation, E = hν. This equation of
modern physics tells that there is some connection between
energy of a system/particle and Planck's constant 'h'. The
Heisenberg's theory of uncertainty as we have already seen
shows that inherent uncertainty of nature or physical reality
is proportional to Planck's constant. Thus, there appears
a linear relation of proportionality between energy of any
system/particle and the amount of uncertainty inherent in
the nature. We may express this chain of relations as:

$$E \sim h \sim \Delta$$

Here '$\sim$' symbolizes connection of proportionality
and 'Δ' symbolizes inherent uncertainty in the nature
(or physical world). Here I am using the general term of
'uncertainty' without specifying 'uncertainty of what'.
This 'Δ' is not specifically the uncertainty of position
or momentum or energy or time but uncertainty-in-
general.... It is the extent to which the physical reality
itself is uncertain. The specific uncertainties viz., that of

position (Δx), momentum (Δp), energy (ΔE) or time (Δt) are nothing but special manifestations of the same general uncertainty in the physical reality of this world. Obviously, 'Δ' is not a specific mathematical quantity and hence no unit of measurement either of position (metre), momentum (kg metre per second), energy (Joule) or time (second) etc., can be attributed to it. Still I am using 'Δ' as I feel that it will be helpful to grasp the general correlations in the structure of cosmic reality we are dealing with.

After precisely defining the physical world and expressing our understanding about this world in the form of above laws of physics, we are in position to list out those parameters of physical reality that play important role in defining and explaining its nature. These parameters are:

1. Space (x y z) or (d)
2. Time (t)
3. Speed (v)
4. Energy (E)
5. Planck's constant (h)
6. Uncertainty-in-general (Δ)

(This may not be an exhaustive list.)

All the six listed parameters are somehow linked with each other. Some of the inter-parameter relations we already know like v = d/t (viz., speed = distance travelled/ time elapsed) and E ~ h ~ Δ. We shall further explore such relations to find that they are leading to the development of a multi-layered structure of cosmic reality and help explaining its various aspects in a unified manner.

There is one more variable that defines a level of reality in its own way. It is consciousness. We have previously discussed about the levels of consciousness and the corresponding levels of reality. To recapitulate, the physical world is the lowest level of consciousness, with zero consciousness. In other words, the objects of physical world e.g., table, chairs, tennis ball are unconscious. Even the bare human body minus sense consciousness, mental consciousness and other higher levels of consciousness is an unconscious material. This becomes obvious on death of a human being. Now, the fact that physical world has zero consciousness is not covered by any law of physics we have discussed. These laws of physics capture some or the other aspect of physical reality and describe the physical world in their own way. Still the contemporary physics misses stating explicitly the fact that this world has zero consciousness. So let us add one more law pertaining to this physical world in the list of laws of physics in form of the following equation:

$$\text{Consciousness} = 0$$

Though this equation is not a part of present day physics but it does represent some characteristic of the physical world and describes the physical reality from that angle. It is notable that in this equation consciousness is used as a parameter that helps in describing the physical reality. Hence, we have to necessarily add consciousness as the seventh parameter in our previous list of six important parameters that are used to describe the physical reality.

(Though I have taken the common sense view that physical systems are non-sentient, the theosophical literatures accord some primal unmanifested consciousness even to them. The 'theory of monads' propounded by **Leibniz** also speaks on similar lines. However, this is not going to interfere with my basic thesis. We can always change the equation of consciousness in physical world equating it to an infinitesimal value instead of zero.)

Space, time, mass and energy—all are the building blocks of physics wrapped in the cloud of definitional and foundational vagueness. They all are like God! We know but we do not know.

For human consciousness, there is a time and space schema. We see everything spaced and timed. It is the way human consciousness is destined to perceive the physical world.

Reference frame is a virtual mathematical construct of a relative perceptual standpoint.

What can be measured by tape can also be measured by clock. It means space and time are not different entities.

Existence of space and time independent of mind is not found, undiscoverable and inexplicable.

We must be thankful to God that the value of Planck's constant 'h' is extremely small in the physical world.

There is some essential elemental uncertainty inherent in the physical world.

No amount of care and precision on the part of measurement can remove this uncertainty, because the quantities of this physical world themselves are intrinsic, though very slightly uncertain in value.

Wave-ness of a matter system gives it some kind of fluidity.

EIGHT

A Physics Beyond the Physics
...Venturing from Known to Unknown

Beyond the world of black and white
Where clarity is illusion 'n' gray is right,
Ignorance of the known and knowledge of unknown
Mixed in a test tube and a baby was grown.

A S I had mentioned at the outset, I want to find way into higher levels of consciousness and reality and discover their character through extension and generalization of basic concepts of physics; its parameters, axioms and laws known with certainty only in the context of physical reality.

Let us start with the physical world that we know through direct perception and which can be described in terms of known parameters with the help of known axioms and laws of physics. This physical world has a natural four-dimensional perceptual scheme of space-time that we know innately and we know that we know. It means the objects and events of this world are observable only in terms of space and time variables. We or say our consciousness knows and feels intrinsically that there is space and time and physics has already educated us that space and time are not different but intrinsically one and the same.

We also know the concept of speed. As I have mentioned previously, this physical world can be defined in terms of speed as world of everything lying in the speed bracket of '0 to c' where 'c' is the speed of light in free space. We also know that every system of the physical world is made up of mass and energy. Physics says that mass and energy are not different but one and the same thing intrinsically. It may be difficult to define the core essence or philosophical meaning of mass and energy but today's physics is fairly able to quantify them in specific units of measurements (e.g., kilogramme and Joule) and apply various formula and equations onto them.

We also know that all the physical systems have dual properties of wave and matter-particle. In addition, physical world has a Planck's constant, which is universal for all the systems of this world...and it is very small in value. We also know that the physical world is inherently uncertain in terms of the boundary precision and values of many of the parameters of its system(s). We even know that the value of Planck's constant is small enough to render this world sufficiently and practically certain for day-to-day life. Lastly, we have also explained this physical world as the one having zero consciousness i.e., its systems and sub-systems are not conscious in the sense we understand consciousness.

My physics is different from contemporary modern physics only in having consciousness as additional parameter fixed at zero value for this world. By switching the knob of this one parameter to non-zero values, my physics is enabled to go beyond the contemporary physics.

Now, let us go above and beyond the Physics. Can we think of a speed higher than the speed of light in free space 'c' i.e., 3×10^8 metre per second? Physics says we cannot while being within the boundaries of the physical world. One underlying assumption of Einstein's theory of relativity is that nothing can move faster than the light in free space. However, the highest speed of the physical world that is 'c' is not the highest thinkable speed; 'c' may be the boundary of physical world but it is not a natural and logical boundary of 'thinkable maximum speed'. If there can be a speed as 3×10^8 metre per second, why cannot there be 3.001×10^8 metre per second or 3.1×10^8 metre per second or 4×10^8 metre per second...and what is wrong in 3×10^{180} metre per second?

Here, I am not referring to the mathematical calculations of electromagnetic theory or the assumptions of special theory of relativity with its known track record of experimental verifications which mandate 'c' as the highest possible speed. I am simply referring to possibilities...natural and logical possibilities. Possibilities always go beyond calculations and experiments. Time and space of the physical world may not be able to contain and sustain the speeds higher than 'c'. However, there may be nothing wrong in conceiving speeds greater than 'c' if we are ready to go beyond the confines of physical world.

While discussing the multi-layered structure of reality we have already assumed and conceived that there exists wide range of realities beyond the physical world. These realities beyond the physical reality may contain and sustain the speeds greater than 'c'.

Having said this, now let us consider these points:

1. As we have already discussed, there is a world of sense consciousness or *Bhuvar lok,* that is just above the physical world or *Bhu lok,* in the multi-layered structure of cosmic reality. The word 'above' simply signifies that it has more consciousness than the physical world. Its systems are slightly sentient while physical systems are completely non-sentient.

2. It is reasonable to think that if the physical world has a speed bracket with highest and lowest speeds ('c and 0'); this world of sense consciousness must also have a speed bracket with its own highest and lowest speeds.

3. Since physical world has zero consciousness and the world of sense level consciousness has some primal consciousness, there cannot be any overlap in the two worlds. It means a system which belongs to the physical world cannot be a part of the world of sense consciousness at the same time. Materially, the two worlds are mutually exclusive.

4. Hence, the world of sense consciousness should start only where the physical world ends. From zero speed up to the speed of light in free space 'c' is the realm of physical world. So we can reasonably assume that beyond 'c' starts the world of sense consciousness.

It means as we go faster than the speed of light in free space 'c', the maximum possible speed in physics, we transcend the physical world and enter into the world of sense consciousness which has its own speed bracket. Logically, the lowest limit of its speed bracket must be just more than 'c', say 'c+', which is practically (almost) equal to 'c'. Now what can be said about the highest limit of the speed bracket of world of sense consciousness...the maximum permissible speed of the world of sense consciousness? We are not able to find its value either logically or mathematically but it must be an extremely high speed...very much higher than 'c', say 'c_1'. Thus, the speed bracket of the world of sense consciousness comes to be 'c+ to c_1'. So this is the range of speeds with which the systems of the world of sense consciousness can move. Now two very fundamental questions may appear to block our ideas:

1. **Is it what that moves?** Speed must be speed of something. What is that something in the world of sense consciousness? When we say that systems of the world of sense consciousness move in speed range 'c + to c_1', of what material these systems are made of?

   In physical world, we have systems of non-sentient matter. Similarly, we may think of sense consciousness itself as sentient substance that constitutes its own world. This substance is not the material substance like matter of physical world. It must be finer, faster, sensible and slightly conscious. It may be observable and capture-able only in its own world. For a human being who is composite of all the levels of consciousness and realities, sentient substance of sense consciousness can only be found or felt or captured by meditative-analytical introspection.

2. **Who is that observer, who sees them moving?** Theory of relativity shows that there is no absolute reference frame. Hence, any account of speed can only be relative to some observer with a reference frame. Now when we say that systems of the world of sense consciousness move in speed range of 'c + to c_1'; this speed bracket must be definable relative to some observer. Who is that observer or set of observers that see(s) systems of sense consciousness moving greater than the speed of light?

My answer runs this way.... Human being as per our model is a composite multi-layered structure of different levels of consciousness including the non-sentient bodily matter. Hence, the human existence participates in all the seven worlds of reality through its different levels of consciousness. However being encumbered with the material body, we objectively think of ourselves as existing in this physical world only. When physics says that we cannot have speed of any physical object greater than 'c', we can translate this fact in the language of our new physics as: 'Human being together with all types of consciousness plus physical body cannot objectively see a speed greater than the speed of light in free space...so long as it is encumbered with physical body.' This is because in this physical world we capture everything objectively.

The notion of relativity of speed is meaningful if we are objective observers seeing things in motion, objectively. However, we can observe speeds greater than 'c' only when we observe subjectively. This happens when our consciousness disengages itself from physical affiliations either by meditative introspection when alive or after death!

Now let us come back to our original chain of thought that is, at speed 'c' physical world ends and beyond 'c' starts the world of sense consciousness. Hence, the transition from non-sentient physical world to world of sense consciousness amounts to transition from lower speed range to higher one. Thus, appears a rough correlation between speed and consciousness.

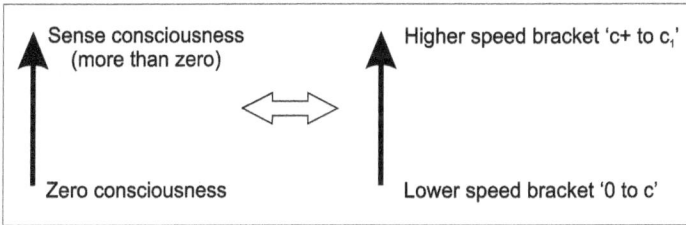

Fig. 8.1   Speed and Consciousness

However, this correlation between speed and consciousness is not smooth but an abrupt one. I mean consciousness of a system does not increase gradually from zero to slightly positive value as we increase the speed from zero upward. Levels of consciousness abruptly change from zero to non-zero (sense level) only after speed crosses a threshold value that is the maximum limit of physical world viz., 'c'. This abruptness in the change in value of some parameters is, as you will see, a peculiar characteristic of this model of multi-layered reality. (Perhaps, the consciousness is also quantized like the energy levels of an atom.)

Recall that speed and consciousness are part of the list of those seven important parameters that play leading role in describing a reality. Other such parameters are space, time, energy, Planck's constant and uncertainty. We can attempt to establish similar correlation between all the important parameters. Some parameters in our list are already correlated by the equations of physics e.g., space, time and speed are correlated by Lorentzian transformation equations and simple equation of speed = distance/time elapsed to cover that distance. Similarly, energy of a system, Planck's constant and uncertainty inherent in the nature are correlated by $E \sim h \sim \Delta$ where '$\sim$' symbolizes connection of proportionality. Now let us try to correlate each of these seven parameters with every other parameter:

The spider-manliness that **K** has shown in weaving the web amongst all the seven parameters of reality is unprecedented. No school of rationalist philosophy has manipulated and fudged our existing knowledge and understanding about the nature so selfishly and ruthlessly as he is going to do. It

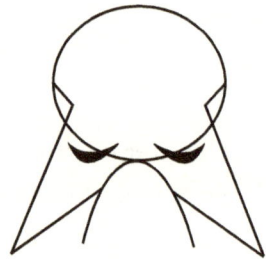

Jampak Zu

is just for pleasure of creation of a knowledge-utopia or conceptual bubble *ex nihilo*. I doubt if there is any creation of new knowledge.

Relation of Time

First of all let us explore the concept of time and its inter-relation with consciousness and speed. Time represents the rate of change in a sequential flux of events. The perception of time is limited to and dependent upon the existence of change. Our breath and metabolic processes are also types of change. They form internal biological clock. Our mental processes also form a type of change. They involve flux of concepts, ideas, percepts etc. They form our mental clock. Apart from the changes in the external world e.g., changes in position of some object or changes in form of a material, the biological and mental clock keeps us conscious of the flux of time inherently.

Now question arises, if all the changes of physical world stop will time stop? I mean if the earth and other planets stop revolving around the sun, the moon stops revolving around the earth, summers and winters, days and nights cease to occur, rivers stop flowing, birds stop flying; human beings, animals and vehicles stop moving, animate world stops breathing, blood stops flowing in veins; everything comes to a standstill and lifeless like a snapshot of a camera, will time stop?... The answer is No!..at least theoretically. Do you know why?... As I have already mentioned, human being is a composite multi-layered structure of different levels of consciousness including the non-sentient bodily matter and hence the human existence participates in all the seven worlds of reality through its different levels of consciousness.

Thus, human existence is not limited to the physical body and its physical life only. Even if the entire physical world comes to dead stop, all physical-biological processes come to a standstill and human body becomes lifeless, the higher levels of human consciousness continue existing and cognizing in their own way.

The death of brain does not mandate annihilation of mental consciousness and other higher consciousnesses. Mind can exist as pure, free and liberated mental consciousness without physicality of brain and so is the case with other higher levels of consciousness e.g., *aham* (I-ness) and soul (pure-I). These levels of consciousness will still recognize the passage of time in their own way. Stoppage of changes in physical world cannot stop changes in the upper levels of consciousness. Since all human beings are equipped with higher levels of consciousness, every free mind, free ego, free soul will perceive time and will also perceive that over passage of this much time, no change in the physical world takes place.

Now take a hypothetical case. What will happen to time if my individual consciousness is annihilated or disappears in totality?… I mean that if somehow not only my physical body but also my mind, my ego and my soul cease to exist, will time stop?… No!..as there are other conscious beings …other human beings with their mind, ego and soul to recognize time. However, time will stop or cease to exist at least for me.

Now, if all the consciousness of all the conscious beings existing at all the levels is annihilated, will time stop?… The answer is…. Yes! A hypothetical 'changeless physical reality' 'in-absence-of-higher-realities' (various levels of consciousness) cannot produce time because then there is nothing to be perceived as timed and no one to perceive. Hence, time is only a perceptional attribute of a changing reality and not a reality-in-itself. This utterly depends on the observed rate of change in reality.

Besides, we have already discussed the topic of time dilation in the theory of special relativity. According to the theory, to an observer a moving clock will tick slowly than a resting clock. Theory mandates that the beat of time or natural rate of succession of events [of physical reality] is not a universal and absolute proposition. It is a relative concept and depends on the speed of observed relative to the observer. There is no time independent of observer and his observation.

In the physical world, various systems have relative speeds in the range of '0 to c'. Depending on the different relative speeds of systems to different observers, a wide spectrum of perception of time will be formed by these observers. When an observer sees some object or event at rest he perceives 'proper time' as it is called in the textbooks of physics. When he observes the same object or event moving, he perceives a beat of time (for that object) slower than the beat of proper time in accordance with the Lorentzian transformation equations [Chaper 7]. When he observes some object or event moving at the speed of light 'c', to him time stops beating for that object/event. This means the object stops ageing and the event stops occurring for the observer.

However, the theory of special relativity with its Lorentzian transformation equations is meant for physical reality only. Lorentzian transformation equations tell us as to how the perceptions of space or distance and time change with change in the relative speed of observer and observed. There is no need to introduce these equations here in their mathematical totality. [Any textbook of modern physics can do this job for the interested readers.]

However, I am putting them in a non-perfectionist form digestible to readers with no significant academic background of physics:

$$\text{Perception of space for speed 'v'} = \frac{\left[\begin{array}{l} \text{Perception of space at zero speed} - \\ \text{v} \times \text{perception of time at zero speed} \end{array} \right]}{\sqrt{1-(v/c)^2}}$$

$$\text{Perception of time for speed 'v'} = \frac{\left[\begin{array}{l} \text{Perception of time at zero speed} - (v/c)^2 \\ \times \text{perception of time at zero speed} \end{array} \right]}{\sqrt{1-(v/c)^2}}$$

These equations will breakdown both conceptually and mathematically as any speed (that is, relative speed of any observed system with respect to any observer) crosses the speed of light in free space i.e., when 'v' exceeds 'c'. As you can see, the above equations are valid only if the speed of any observed system 'v' is less than the speed of light in free space 'c'. As the value of 'v' touches 'c', the term $[1-(v/c)^2]$ becomes zero. Zero in the denominator renders the whole equation mathematically meaningless. If the value of 'v' exceeds 'c' the term $[1-(v/c)^2]$ becomes negative. Even then the root $(\sqrt{\ })$ of a negative number being an imaginary number renders the equation meaningless.

According to our postulations, as we move from physical world to the world of sense consciousness, we actually go from lower speed bracket of '0 to c' to the next higher speed bracket of 'c+ to c_1'.

We have also postulated that a 'Human being together with all types of consciousness plus physical body cannot objectively see a speed greater than the speed of light in free space...so long as it is encumbered with physical body.' So a physical observer (say O) viz., a human being encumbered with physical-material body following these equations may not see the speeds greater than 'c'. We human beings living in this world are like this very physical observer.

However, suppose there is a virtual observer (say O_1) who is stripped off the physical-material body and who can see the systems of the sense consciousness...an observer of higher reality! How will he perceive time?... For him the usual Lorentzian transformation equations will become unusable and will give way to a new, though possibly similar set of equations in which 'c' is replaced by 'c_1', the highest possible speed of the world of sense consciousness.

You can see that if 'c' is replaced by 'c_1', term $[1-(v/c_1)^2]$ does not become zero or negative when the value of 'v' touches or exceeds 'c' because 'c_1' is much greater than 'c'. These will be the new and more generalized Lorentzian type transformation equations that can deal with the world of sense-level consciousness too along with physical world. These equations will be meant for O_1 type of observers.

It is notable that this higher observer O_1 can observe not only the sense-level reality but also the lower reality of physical world but the lower observer O can only see the physical reality. Now following the new Lorentzian-type transformation equations where 'c' is replaced by 'c_1', the higher observer O_1 can calculate the time dilations (slowing of the beat of perceived time with high relative speed) of both the worlds and compare. Thus, O_1 type of observer is best competent for comparing the two worlds. Since the whole range of relative speeds in the world of sense level consciousness is higher than the whole range of that in physical world, O_1 will surely find that the whole range of time in world of sense consciousness is slower than that in the physical world.

Thus for all possible observers who can see both the worlds, the total spectrum of all possible perceptions of time will be slower in the world of sense consciousness than

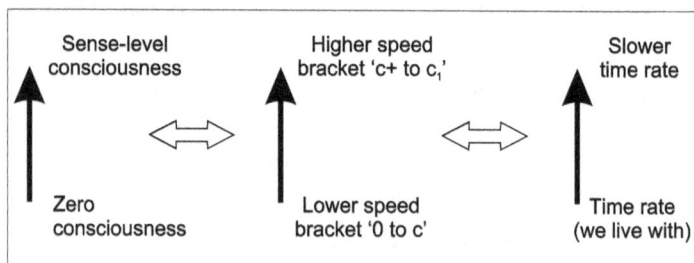

Sense-level consciousness	Higher speed bracket 'c+ to c_1'	Slower time rate
⇔	⇔	
Zero consciousness	Lower speed bracket '0 to c'	Time rate (we live with)

Fig. 8.2 Speed comparison of physical & sense-conscious systems

in the physical world because the observed speeds of sense conscious systems are higher than that of physical systems.

Now we can predict that as we transit from physical world to the world of sense consciousness, there should be an abrupt slowdown in the pace of time in general. Time must beat slowly in the world of sense-level consciousness. Thus, we get another important inter-parameter connection between speed (speed bracket) and time (spectrum of all possible time perceptions) and consciousness.

Relation of Space

Now let us look into the concept of space in depth and explore the inter-relation of space, time and speed. I see a possible connection among these three parameters that is different from conventional approach of a physicist.

Concentrate on the equation, speed = distance travelled/ time elapsed in travelling. The distance is travelled in space. When a particle travels, it traverses and covers various points of the space. The total space represents all possible and available distances for a particle to travel and set of all available points that can be traversed.

Higher the particle speed, more the amount of space or number of points it covers over a given time period. However, a particle cannot move faster than 'c'. This is the limitation of physical reality expressed in terms of the speed in physical world. I want to express the same limitation of physical reality in terms of the space of physical world. So it can be said that any two points of space cannot be touched in sequence faster than 'c'. This statement essentially means that: "Though the space seems to be infinite, the available space for roaming around a space-point over a period of time is always limited due to limitation of speed." Here, I am referring to two more limitations in addition to the limitation of speed in surfing the space:

1. That we are never given unlimited period of time.

2. That we always exist on a space-point and can surf space only around that point.

These limitations do not seem important in first instance but they are. They affect our perception of infinitude of space. Whether space is actually infinite is not known with certainty but our perception of its infinitude rests on the degree of inability to surf the entire space in totality. Space looks infinite as we cannot cover all of it, physically or conceptually. Hence infinitude of space, as we know it, is an indirect and inferential judgment. Whether space is actually infinite is a question beyond our capacity.

Now let us consider three hypothetical cases:

1. A man randomly flying with infinite speed.

2. A man flying with very high speed having infinite age (and infinite memory).

3. A man having innumerable minds which are all connected in real time but distributed spatially over the entire space.

For all the above described three types of hypothetical men, the space may not be 'that infinite' as it is for us or it may not be infinite at all. The perception of infinitude that we have regarding space must not be there in their case. A man randomly flying at infinite speed must be present at all the points of space all the time. For us, his perception about space may be undefined but certainly not 'that infinite' as we have. Similarly, an ageless man with infinite memory moving with high speed who has seen and remembers all the infinite space over the past infinite years of his life may carry perception of finitude or infinitude of space entirely different from us. Also a man whose consciousness is distributed over entire space is present everywhere and sees all space-points simultaneously. For him as well the space may not be finite or infinite in the same way as it is for us. All these three hypothetical examples are presented to make us realize that our idea of infinitude of space rests on our following three limitations:

1. We cannot move at speed more than a certain finite speed 'c' in the physical world.

2. We are never allotted infinite time (with infinite memory) to travel in the space.

3. We at the start of travelling in space or perceiving space, are always at one space-point and can at the maximum move or see only around that point.

I call the above three as 'factors of limitation'. We actually never see the space as infinite as we cannot see infinite. We see only local space, finite space and limited space. Infinitude of space is our inference from our perception and natural logic. Hence, infinitude of space is an 'inferential attribute' that we ascribe to space. These factors of limitation limit our perception of space and give rise to 'perceptional finitude' of space on one hand and inferential feeling of infinitude of space on the other.

I think if any one of the three factors of limitation is removed somehow, say by divine magic, the liberated human perception can then capture the infinitude of space directly. The space then will not be inferentially infinite but perceptually infinite to human consciousness (provided it is actually infinite!... And that we do not know with certainty). However, it is a hypothetical issue. So let us not waste time on it.

.... And what about the time of reader that has already been wasted in reading this all? I do not think that this much of deliberation is required to establish the simple point that infinitude of space is an inferential judgment and not a perceptual one. It has to be that way. You cannot directly perceive the infinitude! Can you? Putting a simple concept in so many words cannot make it great.

Jampak Zu

Now a question arises—Which space we should take as our authentic parameter to define physical reality. The unlimited space to which we ascribe attribute of infinitude inferentially or the local space that is approachable, accessible and covered or easily coverable by perception. The latter is limited, though its limits are vague, by definition. They depend on the duration of observation, which is a matter of choice or chance. So we may state that there is inferentially infinite space but out of it only perceivably limited space is available for enquiry at a given moment of time. Since unlimited space is an unchanging and constant proposition, I prefer to take approachable and traceable local space as the parameter that defines a reality or say real systems. I used so many words only to introduce the concept of limited and available space.

To revisit, as we move from the physical world to the world of sense consciousness, we translate from lower speed bracket of 'zero to c' to higher speed bracket of 'c+ to c_1'. We have seen that time beats slower at higher speeds. So time passes slowly in the world of sense-level consciousness compared to the physical world. Hence, a moving system in the world of sense consciousness can traverse or cover much more space than a physical system in the physical world during the equivalent time period.

Recall here the famous example of muons that we had discussed under the topics of 'time dilation' and 'length contraction' in Einstein's theory of relativity. To an observer on earth time dilates for fast moving muon and it is able to cover a distance over 6,000 metres before decaying which otherwise could cover only 600 metres. Similarly, to an observer time beats slower for the fast moving systems of world of sense-level consciousness than that in the physical world. Hence, the system of sense-level consciousness covers more distance compared to what a physical system may cover in the equivalent time in the physical world. In other words, for sense-level conscious system the available or perceivable or coverable or traceable space is always more vis-à-vis a physical system.

However, we are coming to this conclusion as an external observer. I mean that we are looking at the systems in different worlds as if we are not the part of these systems. We can call this type of observation as 'external observer's point of view'. So here, our position is similar to the observer attached to the earth that sees the fast moving muon. What shall we conclude if we ourselves are the system(s), physical or sense-level conscious system (or attached to the system)? This likens asking as if what an observer attached to a fast moving muon will conclude. This second type of observation may be called 'system's point of view'.

We have seen under the topic of 'length contraction' in Einstein's theory of relativity that muon or a virtual observer attached to muon will see itself covering only 600 metres before touching the earth's surface. However to an observer attached to the earth, the muon actually covers a distance over 6,000 metres. Thus for a fast moving observer like muon, the coverable or traceable distance contracts. So a fast moving muon approaching the earth will see the earth within 600 metres only while to the observer on earth muon is actually 6,000 metres away. Thus the long distance of 6,000 metres shrinks into the limited and available distance of 600 metres for the muon. It means that for fast moving observers (viz., as per system's point of view) the space shrinks just like a compressible substance and hence more amount of space comes under their purview as limited coverable or available space!!!

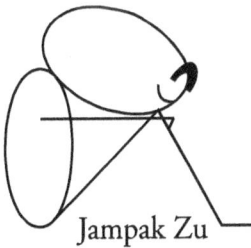

Jampak Zu

Will you all still like to continue???

This may not be easy to understand and appreciate for all readers. Let us understand it graphically. Figure 8.3 depicts

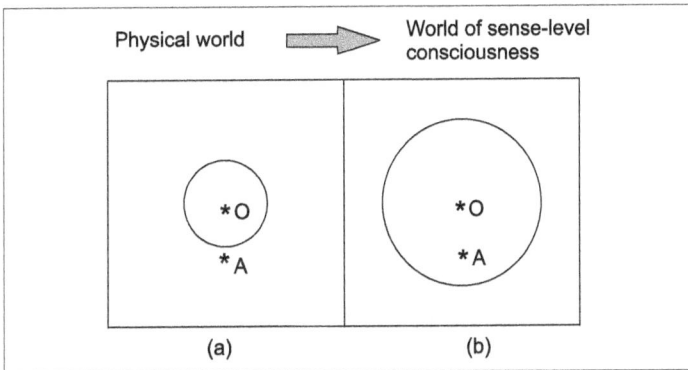

Fig. 8.3   Limited perceivable space (roughly/vaguely) at some space-time point 'O' (x y z t) in (a) Physical world and (b) World of sense-level consciousness

change in space perception in transition from physical world to the world of sense-level consciousness:

The two rectangular boxes symbolize the infinite space of two different worlds: one for physical world and the other for world of sense-level consciousness. Though pictorially, the rectangles shown have defined boundaries, we may assume that the rectangles are infinitely large with no perceivable boundaries. (They are like the infinite universe of set theory). There is a common point O in both the rectangles. O in the rectangle of the physical world represents some point in the space and time of physical world. In the second rectangle, O represents same or similar point defined in terms of space and time of the world of sense consciousness. There is a circle around point O in both the rectangles. These circle-in-the-rectangle symbolize the limited space available and accessible to and coverable by a point system (e.g., a particle) located at space-time point O in a given interval of time.

If a randomly moving particle is instantaneously located at point O at a moment of time 't', the maximum available space for access to this particle during the time interval Δt (which is in the vicinity of point of time 't') will be a sphere of radius 'cΔt' around point O. This is so because the particle can traverse the maximum distance of 'cΔt' (maximum distance = maximum possible speed × time interval given) in any direction away from point O. It cannot go beyond this sphere of radius 'cΔt' of which O is the centre.

Practically and numerically, the concept of available or

accessible space is quite vague as neither the duration of moment Δt is defined nor all the systems of the physical world are truly point systems. Everything from duration of moment Δt and size of system to its speed and direction is a matter of choice or chance. Reality is very complicated and hence the 'limited available space' is quantitatively not a defined parameter. It is important at concept level only to bring out the fact that the space that we capture for any enquiry is never the infinite stretch of space but only limited available space which is subject to changes as we change the speed brackets or worlds.

In Figure 8.3, there is some point 'A' in universal infinite space which is out of the circle of limited available space. As we move from the physical world to the world of sense-level consciousness, the limited, accessible or coverable or available space increases. The circle representing the limited space enlarges and covers say the point 'A' that was previously outside. We are looking at the systems and the inter-world transitions as an outsider and external observer.

Now let us get back to the original question. What shall we observe if we ourselves are the system(s), physical or sense-level conscious system (or attached to the system)? From systems point of view, the observation must be different. There is a fundamental tenet of relativity that an observer never observes the changes in/motions of the frame of reference to which it is attached. In ideal conditions, you in a moving train will never notice the motion of train. The train is fixed for you. You only observe the motion of trees etc., in opposite direction. You always project the motions/changes of your reference-frame outward, separate from itself (reference-frame) and yourself.

Similarly from system's point of view, a transition from physical world to world of sense-level consciousness will not result in enlargement of the circle of limited available space. That circle is fixed for observer attached to the system. However then, how to account for more space being available and accessible? I mean how to account for point 'A' coming into the purview of limited available space? (For muon's example it is like asking that how the earth's surface which is 6,000 metres away comes under the purview of muon's accessibility of 600 metres.) From system's angle, there will only be compression of space into seemingly constant circle of limited accessible and available space. Compression of space means more space out of infinite universal space that will come under the purview/circle of coverage, accessibility and availability. We may represent it

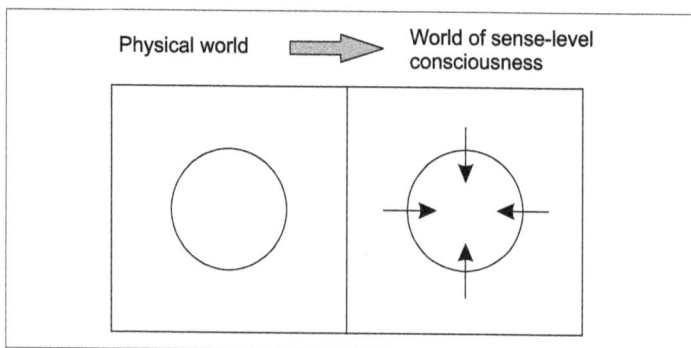

Fig. 8.4 Compression of space relative to system itself; meaning of all symbols remaining the same

graphically as in Figure 8.4.

Inward arrows in the right hand side of the figure show that more and more space comes into the purview of limited available space of a system as we move from the physical world to the world of sense consciousness. So if the same system is to jump from low speed bracket of the physical world to high speed bracket of the world of sense consciousness, the observer attached to it will observe that the space gets compressed and becomes denser i.e., the distance between any two points in space decreases. Space reduces from system's point of view. Since there is no observer in the world whose consciousness is unattached to one or the other system of the world, (our body also is a system) the observation from system's point of view regarding the space is the only perception available to human intellect. Thus for all practical purposes, we may conclude that space as we perceive it gets compressed, shrinks inward, shortens and gets denser as we translate from the physical world to the world of sense consciousness.

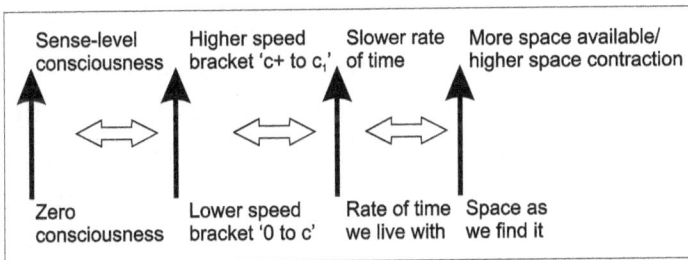

| Sense-level consciousness | Higher speed bracket 'c+ to c_1,' | Slower rate of time | More space available/ higher space contraction |
| Zero consciousness | Lower speed bracket '0 to c' | Rate of time we live with | Space as we find it |

Fig. 8.5   Relation between space, speed, time and consciousness

Well, now I feel that I am in position to establish inter-parameter connection between space, speed and time…and hence, consciousness as well.

Thus when we move from the physical level of zero consciousness to the level of sense consciousness, translating to higher speed bracket, the time slows down and the space expands from external observer's point of view (or shrinks from system's point of view). It brings more space per space to the observer.

Relation of Planck's constant

By now we have established inter-parameter connection between four vital parameters of our analysis viz., consciousness, speed, time and space. Now the left out parameters are energy (E), Planck's constant (h) and uncertainty-in-general (Δ). Let us first explore the concept and full import of uncertainty. As we have already discussed, (during the discussion on Heisenberg's uncertainty principle) uncertainty is the very characteristic of the nature that the God has made or caused.

There is uncertainty in the position of systems, their momentum, their energy, time etc. This uncertainty is not due to our inability to measure them precisely. Rather the nature (which must include all the worlds) and its parameters are inherently and structurally uncertain to some extent. We have seen (in Chapter 7) that these inherent and structural uncertainties are to a large extent explained by recourse to concept of wave-particle duality and matter waves.

De Broglie's hypothesis (every moving body in certain ways exhibits character of waves) is the pillar of concept of wave-particle duality. It is very simple and general in nature. It applies to all types of physical systems…be it a moving rocket, bullet shot, high speed electron or photon.

The waves associated with or exhibited by or equivalent to any moving system of matter are called 'matter waves' or 'de Broglie waves'. So we may say that a moving rocket, a zooming bullet or a high speed electron are nothing but a set of matter waves. Every wave has some wavelength and so do matter waves. To have a wavelength is conventionally peculiar to wave. Similarly, every moving matter system has some momentum which is the product of mass of system and its speed. To have momentum is conventionally peculiar to matter systems. De Broglie proposed an equation which relates wavelength of matter waves 'λ' with momentum of a moving system 'mv' and Planck's constant 'h' as:

$$\lambda = h/mv$$

To put it in other way:

$$\lambda \times mv = h$$

Here 'mv' is the momentum of a system wherein 'v' is the speed and 'm' is the mass of system. The beauty of de Broglie's equation lies in its mathematical simplicity with which it relates a peculiar parameter of wave with a peculiar parameter of matter particle establishing wave-particle duality.

If the speed of a system 'v' is increased, its momentum 'mv' will also increase. As 'h' is constant for the whole physical world, according to de Broglie's equation the increase in speed and hence momentum will result in decrease in wavelength 'λ' of the system. We have seen that wave-ness associated with every moving matter system renders the later some kind of spread-ness.

Since wavelength 'λ' is the length of one matter wave (or de Broglie wave) attached to a moving system, we may say that 'λ' roughly signifies the spread of the system on axis of motion when we see a moving system in terms of wave characters. To the extent a matter system spreads we have some probability of finding matter. We may state the same fact in other way round that a moving matter system spreads to the extent there is some (non-zero) probability of finding matter.

So if speed of matter system 'v' is high, wavelength 'λ' will be less which in turn implies that spread of system will be less. Hence, there will be smaller range over the axis of motion having some probability of finding matter of that system. Obviously, the uncertainty of position of the system on the axis of motion will also be low. Thus, wavelength of matter wave 'λ' is in rough proportionality with uncertainty in position. High 'λ' means high 'Δ' and low 'λ' signifies low 'Δ'.

(Some of you may note that presently I am confining my parameter of general uncertainty 'Δ' to uncertainty of position or space only because for the time being I am going to concentrate on the role of 'λ' in developing the subject and it is a space parameter i.e., measurable in space units.)

Now we have a linkage—higher the speed, higher is the momentum, then lower will be the wavelength and lower the uncertainty.

We have discussed earlier that uncertainty in a system is due to the wave-ness of every moving system. Now what I am going to tell you is a layman's explanation of relation in 'λ', 'v' and 'Δ'. To be frank, it has nothing to do with the positivistic correctness in the eyes of a student of modern physics. Suppose there is a moving system of length 'L' along the axis of motion. The speed of system is 'v' and the mass is 'm'.

Suppose there is only one matter wave associated with that moving system. (These assumptions are too simplistic to be true...anyway). Let the wavelength of this one wave be 'λ'. Since 'λ' signifies the spread of the system wherein some

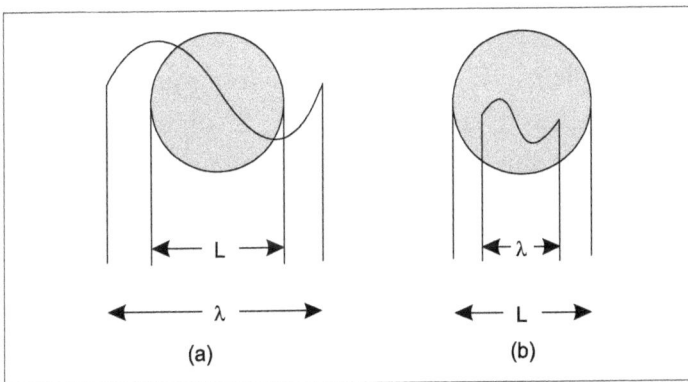

Fig. 8.6 Wavelength of matter wave and uncertainty in position
(a) Position of spread out (b) Not possible

probability of finding matter of that system will always exist, 'λ' will always be more than 'L'. Since 'L' is the length of the system in terms of particle-character, this 'L' must be fully covered by 'λ'. If we take 'λ' less than 'L', in the portion of 'L–λ' there will be some moving matter without associated wave which is impossible according to wave-particle duality. Hence 'λ' must be greater than or equal to 'L'. The portion 'λ–L' is roughly the "possible spread-out of matter" which signifies the degree of uncertainty in position. (Refer to Figure 8.6 where point D is in this 'λ–L' portion only.)

According to de Broglie's equation, we have seen that as we increase the speed of the physical system, 'λ' decreases. Hence for specific 'L', the quantity 'λ–L' which roughly signifies the uncertainty of boundary location also decreases. What will happen if we go on increasing the speed of the system?... 'λ' and 'λ–L' will go on decreasing. The maximum permissible speed for a physical system is that of light in free space 'c'. What will happen if we increase the speed of a physical system up to 'c' (which is practically not possible)?... 'λ' will shrink up to its minimum possible value which is 'L' itself. In any case, 'λ' cannot be smaller than 'L'. At this point 'λ–L' will become zero. It means uncertainty of position will be zero.

This explanation is not true for photon. Photon is fundamentally different from all other physical systems, as it has no 'L' but only 'λ'. Hence, its uncertainty in position cannot be defined by 'λ–L'. Even at the speed of 'c' it will have uncertainty in position.

Now the million dollar question arises—As we translate from physical world to the world of sense consciousness, all things including the laws of nature remaining the same, what will happen to 'λ'? This translation beyond the physical world means crossing the limit of speed of light in free space viz., 'c'.

If de Broglie's equation is to work even beyond the physical world, for which I do not see any reason against, as speed 'v' becomes more than 'c', 'λ' should shrink smaller than 'L'. However, 'λ' cannot be smaller than 'L'. How to resolve the problem?... Do you have any answer?... I think, I have.

Now the remaining and still unexplored parameter of de Broglie's equation is Planck's constant. For the physical world it is a universal constant. However, now it has to change to resolve this problem.

Let us assume that as we translate from the physical world to the world of sense-level consciousness, the Planck's constant jumps to quite higher value. It means the Planck's constant of the world of sense-level consciousness is appreciably higher than Planck's constant of the physical world. As you know, the latter is denoted by 'h'. Let us denote the former by 'h_1'. So $h_1 \gg h$. The symbol '$\gg$' denotes that h_1 is very high in value as compared to h. Now de Broglie's equation in the world of sense-level consciousness will take form as given below:

$$\lambda_1 \times mv = h_1$$

In the above formulae, 'λ_1' is the wavelength of the system in the world of sense-level consciousness assuming that sense-conscious systems also exhibit wave-particle duality in their own way.

At the transition point of the physical world to the world of sense-level consciousness, speed on the either side of the point is in the vicinity of 'c' or 'c+'. So at this transition point, momentum 'mv' does not change much. Hence, with big jump in the value of Planck's constant from 'h' to 'h_1', as per de Broglie's equation, wavelength 'λ' becomes enormously high (to which I have denoted 'λ_1'). It means during transition a sudden expansion of wave associated with the moving system takes place. Now there remains no question of 'λ' getting smaller than 'L' as speed goes beyond 'c'. Beyond 'c' the whole scene changes!

We can assume that in the world of sense-level consciousness too, as we go on increasing the speed, again 'λ_1' goes on shrinking as per de Broglie's equation. However, 'λ_1' always remains sufficiently high and in no case is less than 'L'. So our assumption that as we move into a higher world—from the physical world to the world of sense-level consciousness, Planck's constant increases heavily in step, resolves the problem and it seems digestible too.

Digestible to whom?...
K or the reader?

Jampak Zu

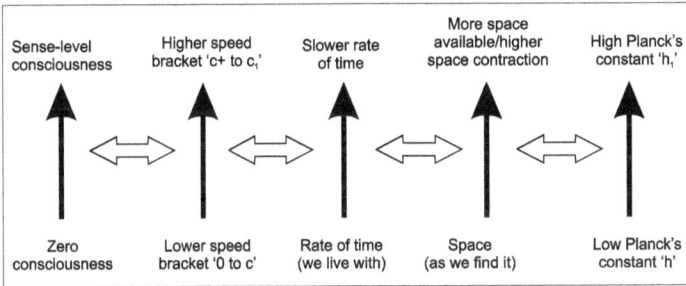

Fig. 8.7 Relation between space, speed, time, consciousness and Planck's constant

We may hence take it as a fact for our model. So Planck's constant is not constant in the universal scheme of which physical world is only a part. It is only constant for the physical world. Now we may include Planck's constant in our inter-parameter linkage.

Relation of Uncertainty

We have just discussed that transition from the physical world to the world of sense-level consciousness dramatically enhances 'λ'. This results in shooting of the value of 'λ–L'; a quantity that roughly signifies uncertainty in position. Our analysis of de Broglie's equation at the inter-world transition point shows that speed 'v' remains in the vicinity of 'c'. Only 'λ' and 'h' change appreciably.

Interestingly, this conceptual picture is verifiable by Heisenberg's uncertainty principle. We know that uncertainty principle is given as:

$$\Delta x \Delta p \approx h/2\pi$$

Here, 'Δx' is uncertainty in position which according to my model corresponds to 'λ–L'. Δp is uncertainty in momentum. With increase in 'λ', uncertainty in position 'λ–L' also jumps high.

If Planck's constant shoots high at inter-world transition point, the total uncertainty product ($\Delta x \Delta p$) and hence one or both of its parts (Δx and Δp) must also go up in value. I could not find any reason in heavy jump of 'Δp'. However, jump in 'Δx' is explainable because in transition from physical world to world of sense consciousness, 'λ' and hence 'λ–L' too go high. Thus our analysis of de Broglie's equation at the transition point is also corroborated by Heisenberg's uncertainty principle.

Jump in the value of 'h' is an important thing as 'h' represents uncertainty. We had discussed earlier that the physical world we live in is almost certain because here 'h' is very small. Any enhancement in the value of 'h' will make the world more uncertain. So having said this, in this

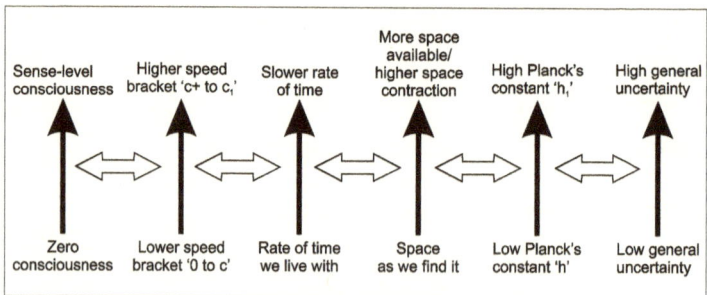

Sense-level consciousness	Higher speed bracket 'c+ to c_i'	Slower rate of time	More space available/ higher space contraction	High Planck's constant 'h,'	High general uncertainty
⬆	⬆	⬆	⬆	⬆	⬆
⬌	⬌	⬌	⬌	⬌	
⬆	⬆	⬆	⬆	⬆	⬆
Zero consciousness	Lower speed bracket '0 to c'	Rate of time we live with	Space as we find it	Low Planck's constant 'h'	Low general uncertainty

Fig. 8.8   Relation between space, speed, time, consciousness Planck's constant and uncertainty

model as we move from the physical world to the world of sense-level consciousness, the total uncertainty product or 'uncertainty-in-general' should enhance heavily. Thus, the world of sense-level consciousness must be structurally more uncertain than the physical world. Now we may include 'uncertainty-in-general' in our general inter-parameter linkage as given in Figure 8.8.

Relation of Energy

Now, let us concentrate on Planck's equation of energy of a physical system: $E=h\nu$; where 'E' is the energy of the system and 'ν' is the frequency of the wave associated with the system. Students of physics know that $\nu=c/\lambda$ where 'c' is the speed of light in free space, and 'λ' is the wave length. Here, 'c' is the upper limit of speed in the speed bracket of the physical world (which ranges from '0 to c'). Can we think of a speed bracket for the world of sense-level consciousness too?...Why not. We have already discussed that the speed bracket of the world of sense-level consciousness starts with c+ which is just above c.

We may assume an upper limit of speed for this world as say c_1 which must be very high over c or c+. So the speed bracket of the world of sense-level consciousness will be c+ to c_1.

If we have to formulate a Planck's equation for the energy of a system of a sense-level conscious system, it must be like:

$$E_1 = h_1\, c_1/\lambda_1$$

Here as a thumb rule, I have just replaced all the parameters of Planck's equation by their "other world counterparts". Hence, 'c' is replaced by the upper limit of speed in the world of sense-level consciousness viz., 'c_1'. And 'E_1' is roughly the energy of a sense-level conscious system assuming that Planck's like law works even beyond the physical world, for which I do not find any reason against.

Now let us compare the Planck's equations of the two different worlds—the physical world and the world of sense-level consciousness.

$$E = hc/\lambda \qquad E_1 = h_1 c_1 / \lambda_1$$

Here, $h_1 >> h$ and $c_1 >> c$ and also $\lambda_1 >> \lambda$.

It means at inter-world transition point, all the three parameters on the right hand side of Planck's equation jump up heavily. Here, assume that the jumping is in proportion. Since two parameters are in numerator and only one in denominator, there must be net increase in the energy of a system as we translate from physical world to the world of sense-level consciousness. Hence, we can justifiably state that world of sense-level consciousness and its systems are

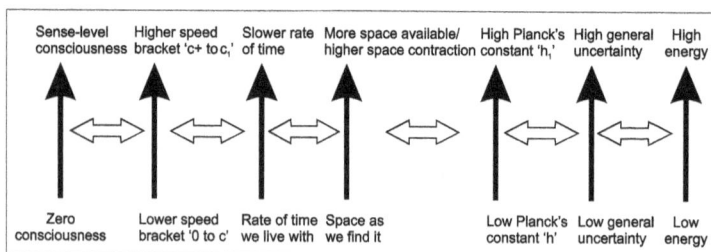

Fig. 8.9   Relation between space, speed, time, consciousness
Planck's constant, uncertainty and energy

It means that for fast moving observers (viz., as per system's point of view) the space shrinks just like a compressible substance and hence more amount of space comes under their purview as limited coverable or available space!!!

Time and space of the physical world may not be able to contain and sustain the speeds higher than 'c'. However, there may be nothing wrong in conceiving speeds greater than 'c' if we are ready to go beyond the confines of physical world.

'Human being together with all types of consciousness plus physical body that cannot objectively see a speed greater than the speed of light in free space...so long as it is encumbered with physical body.'

Whether space is actually infinite is not known with certainty but our perception of its infinitude rests on the degree of inability to surf the entire space in totality.

"Though the space seems to be infinite, the available space for roaming around a space-point over a period of time is always limited due to limitation of speed."

Time is only a perceptional attribute of a changing reality and not a reality-in-itself.

Higher the speed, higher is the momentum, then lower will be the wavelength and lower the uncertainty.

Human being as per our model is a composite multi-layered structure of different levels of consciousness including the non-sentient bodily matter.

We never see the space as infinite as we cannot see infinite.

For sense-level conscious system, the available or the perceivable or the coverable or traceable space is always more vis-à-vis a physical system.

far more energetic than the physical world and its systems. I think that the upper world is a high energy zone compared to this world. Now we are able to extend our inter-parameter linkage covering energy as well.

However, here lies a rider. We may not claim that every system of the world of sense consciousness has more energy than all the systems of physical world because energy of a system depends on how we define a system...what is the type and the boundary of system. My system under enquiry may be a star or a tennis ball. Former has higher energy than the latter. Similarly, there must be different systems in the world of sense-level consciousness. So, we may not compare a big system of physical system with a small sense-conscious system to claim that the latter necessarily has higher energy than the former. So I think, systems to compare should be equivalent. Besides, there are conceptual challenges regarding how we can set equivalence. Also we do not know whether there is any difference in the meaning and the structure of energy in the two worlds. Anyway, something must be left for the readers also.

For me this inter-parameter linkage chain is complete now. You may add more aspects to it. If you recall, I had listed seven important parameters of reality before starting our analysis of inter-world transition. They were—space, time, speed, consciousness, Planck's constant, uncertainty and energy. Now we know a general trend of how all these seven parameters will change if we traverse from the physical world up to the world of sense-level consciousness.

NINE

A Journey Beyond This World
...To a Destination from Where
Every Traveller Starts

Beyond what discovered in scientific way,
Beyond all beliefs the sages say,
I wanna be again what I am,
I wanna go back where I stay.

*I*N OUR initial discussion, while analysing the mind, ego (I-ness) and soul (pure-I), we had chalked out seven worlds—one stacked on the other in the order of increasing consciousness. Now I shall hypothetically traverse all the seven worlds starting from the physical world (*Bhu lok*) at the bottom, up to the world of pure consciousness (*Adi lok*) at the top. I shall then extrapolate the general trend of changes in all the seven parameters that we found in transition from the physical world to the world of sense consciousness. I assume that the trend of change for all the parameters of reality remains the same at all the inter-world transition points. We never know the reality but this is the most probable and reasonable hypothesis, if nature is not chaos up to finality.

So let us traverse from the world of sense consciousness to the world of mental consciousness (*Manomaya lok*). In our earlier analysis of self-consciousness, it is shown that the mental consciousness is higher, more powerful, vivid and refined than the sense-level consciousness. Latter is only the primal animalistic consciousness while mental consciousness has power to apprehend, conceive and synthesize. In technical parlance, systems belonging to the world of mental consciousness possess higher consciousness than the systems belonging to the world of sense consciousness.

Now, in terms of speed, the world of sense consciousness is defined as a set of all the systems having speed in the range of c+ to c_1. Here, c_1 is the upper limit of the world of sense consciousness. So as the speed of a system goes beyond c_1, say becomes c_1+ which is just higher than c_1, the system comes to belong to the world of mental consciousness. As the upper speed limit of world of sense consciousness viz., c_1 is appreciably higher than that of physical world viz., c, the upper speed limit of the world of mental consciousness (say it c_2) must be much higher than c_1. Thus in terms of speed, the world of mental consciousness can be defined as a set of all systems having speed in the range 'c_1+ to c_2'. Thus, as we traverse from the world of sense-level consciousness to the world of mental consciousness, we actually translate from a lower speed bracket of 'c+ to c_1' to higher speed bracket of 'c_1+ to c_2'.

Similarly, all other parameters will change at the inter-world transition point from the world of sense consciousness to the world of mental consciousness as we found them changing while traversing from the physical world to the world of sense consciousness. Time will beat slower for the mental world compared to the world of sense consciousness. Available/accessible space will expand from external observer's point of view, and from system's point of view there will be further contraction of space in this transition. There must be a different Planck's constant for the world of mental consciousness, say h_2 which is much higher than h_1...the Planck's constant for world of sense-level consciousness. 'Uncertainty-in-general' or 'Δ' must also be higher in former vis-à-vis latter. It means the world of mental consciousness is fundamentally more uncertain and wavy or fluid than the world of sense consciousness. In the former, the probability of finding any system is spread over much larger geographical space than in latter.

Similarly, the general energy levels of world of mental consciousness are much higher than that in the world of sense consciousness. Thus, the systems in the world of mental consciousness are finer, faster, observe slower time rate and larger accessible space, are more energetic but also more uncertain and wavy than the systems of world of sense consciousness. Above all they are more conscious too!

The next level of consciousness above mental one is that of 'I-ness' or *aham* (ego). It is the consciousness of 'I' stripped of body and mind predicates. It is individual's subjective identity as a person. It is that identity which when carries body, senses and mind gives rise to objectively accessible and complete person-hood. What will happen as we move from the world of mental consciousness to the world of I-consciousness or simply 'I-ness'? We may predict similar changes in all the seven parameters. Consciousness of 'I' is more concentrated, powerful and finer than mental consciousness. Again we may assume that there must be a upper limit to the speed for the world of 'I-ness'. Say it is c_3. So the world of 'I-ness' can be defined as one encompassing all the systems in the speed range of 'c_2+ to c_3', where c_2+ is just above c_2. (c_2 is the maximum speed of world of mental consciousness.) This speed range must be extremely high compared to the lower worlds.

Again as we traverse from the world of mental consciousness to the world of 'I-ness', in the latter, time will move even slower, space will contract even more (from system's point of view), Planck's constant of this world (say h_3) will be even higher than h_2, uncertainty-in-general will be more and general energy level of systems in the world of 'I-ness' will be very high compared to the world of mental consciousness.

In a nutshell, the systems belonging to the world of I-consciousness must not only be finer, more conscious, faster, energetic, observing slower rate of time, with more perceivable space, but also have more uncertain spread and be wavy in nature compared to systems of the world of mental consciousness.

The next higher level of consciousness above the consciousness of 'I' or ego is that of 'pure-I'. It is the self-consciousness stripped of 'I-ness' or ego. It is the consciousness of soul or the soul itself. Soul is the system of such consciousness. It is pure consciousness... extremely vivid, very strong, fine and concentrated. Here, the level of consciousness is almost infinite.

The speed bracket of the world of 'pure-I' consciousness may be assumed to be from 'c_3+ to c_4'. Here, c_4 is the upper limit of speed for this world. So the world of 'pure-I' may be defined as the set of systems having speed from c_3+ to c_4. This speed range must be too high for human intellect to comprehend. The c_4 can be taken as extremely high speed but yet not infinite.

Following the general trend of inter-world transition when we traverse from the world of 'I-ness' to the world of 'pure-I', the time-rate drops to infinitesimally slow rate! Space contracts (from system's point of view) so heavily that 'almost' all the space is available at a point rendering every system-point a microcosm! However from external observer's point of view, we may say that at such high speed the systems of the world of 'pure-I' move so fast at random that almost all the space is accessible, traceable and available to them. They exist almost everywhere!

At the inter-world transition, the value of Planck's constant also shoots up almost approaching infinitude. So the Planck's constant for the world of 'pure-I' say h_4 must be extremely higher than h_3. Uncertainty-in-general of systems of this world must also be incomprehensibly high…higher than the uncertainty of world of 'I-ness'.

This conclusion also gets corroboration from the effect of inter-world transition on space from external observer's viewpoint. If we accept that almost all the space is available and coverable in the speed range and time-rate of the world of 'pure-I'; the systems of this world exist almost everywhere, and almost all the time. The systems which are so much spread must have incomprehensible level of uncertainty-in-general. Lastly, the systems of the world of 'pure-I' must be almost infinitely energetic.

Though this account of conscious systems of the world of 'pure-I' seems mystical and incomprehensible, it can better be understood as the stage of a universal trend of parameters where things have gone out of direct human intelligibility... however, the account is indirectly comprehensible...by extrapolation of the intelligible.

What next to the world of 'pure-I'? There is a world of available God or super soul as we had discussed in our model of reality. However, I could not capture this level of reality simply by stepwise peel-off analysis of consciousness. I placed it in my model only to align it to the models of theosophy and also to acknowledge the popular deliberations on the available versus the actual God.

Strictly speaking, on my scale of consciousness just above the level of consciousness of 'pure-I' there is ultimate level of pure consciousness. It is 'consciousness-as-such'. One difference in consciousness of 'pure-I' and pure consciousness is that the compass of the former is narrower covering one's self-consciousness stripped of all 'I-ness' and predicative encumbrances. However, the latter has infinite compass...it is infinite 'consciousness-as-such'...better say...He is infinite 'consciousness-as-such'. This is the highest level of consciousness in terms of magnitude, strength and refinement. This is the (actual) God or *Brahma* of *Vedanta* or somewhat like *Drashta* of *Samkhya* or ultimate reality. God is the infinite conscious system. This system constitutes a world of its own…world of pure consciousness or *Adi lok*. Finite human intellect or the intellect of a physicist cannot comprehend the infinitude of pure consciousness. However, the pure consciousness can comprehend all things (realized or potential) at one and the same time.

What about the speed, time and space in the world of pure consciousness? It is incomprehensible but we may logically extrapolate the inter-world trends of parameters and can come to some conclusion by reason. These reasoned conclusions may help in describing the system of pure consciousness or God more closely.

In our model of multi-layered reality, consciousness has direct correlation of proportionality with speed of system(s). So the infinite consciousness can only correspond to infinite speed. Well, the system of pure consciousness stands at (or say runs at) the speed that is infinity. This speed is mathematically incomprehensible.

In mathematics, a variable can never be said to be equal to infinity ($x = \infty$); at the most it may tend to infinity ($x \to \infty$). What is the significance and the import of infinite speed? Pure conscious system is randomly traversing all the space with infinite speed. It means that the system is literally present everywhere! Everywhere means everywhere…at all the points of space-time. Here, there is no scope of 'almost' …no blind spot. It is omnipresent God!

Similarly, at this level the rate of time drops to zero. Its import is dramatic. Time stops and hence effectively there remains no time flux. In lower worlds, a moving system may be at location x_1 at time t_1 and move to location x_2 at time t_2. However, the Godly system of pure consciousness moves with infinite fastness from x_1 to x_2 and reaches at x_2 at same time t_1 only without letting the time perception change. All the changes in space perception occurs at the same time with zero change in time perception. Time shrinks to one point. However, 'still time' is a meaningless notion. The level of pure consciousness is thus timeless. There is no time to refer to. In fact, the account of space as just given for pure consciousness is also not absolutely correct. In absence of time we cannot say that Godly system traverses all the space with infinite speed. With no time there can be no traversing, change or possibility of change. Hence, no concept of space can stand in the world of pure consciousness. It is all just pure consciousness with no objective time and space. To finite human intellect it is bizarre!

Similar extrapolations can be done for other parameters too, such as uncertainty, Planck's constant and general energy level of systems of the world of pure consciousness. Following the trend of variations, we may say that all these three parameters will go infinite in this world. Otherwise also at extreme speed of infinity, everything should be uncertain. At this speed the spread of matter waves (call them 'waves of existence') will also be infinite covering all the infinite space (from external observer's point of view).

With infinite uncertainty-in-general, Planck's constant will also go infinite. This renders Heisenberg's equations incomprehensibly correct viz., $\infty = \infty$.

As energy levels are proportional to Planck's constant, we may conclude that Godly system of pure consciousness is infinitely energetic. It is omnipotent God!

The account of God or purely conscious system that we have found by parametric extrapolation of universal trends of variations describes Him to be an omniscient, omnipresent, omnipotent, unchanging, incomprehensible reality where space-time conception becomes absurd. Since human mind is destined to think in terms of time and space, the actual God by default is out of the purview of our intellect. We cannot capture or find Him; we may only reason Him out. Even mathematically, any variable or parameter equating infinity is an incomprehensible situation.

So the actual God or pure consciousness is incomprehensible even to mathematics that can only handle variables tending to infinity but not the ones equal to infinity. Even situation of 'tending to infinity' is directly incomprehensible to human intellect but mathematically it is comprehensible…and mathematics is only an extension of direct human conceivability.

Well, this is not the end of the thesis I had initially set to develop. There is a technical blind spot in it. We saw that the speed bracket of the world of 'pure-I' was c_3+ to c_4 where c_4 is extremely high though not infinity. However, the speed of Godly system is infinity. There comes a gap on the scale of speed from c_4 to infinity (∞). Sense of continuity demands that there must be a world of systems having speed range from c_4+ to 'speed tending to infinity'. Here c_4+ is a speed just above c_4. This speed bracket is quite different from other speed brackets of other worlds in that its one end is finite speed and other end is incomprehensibly never ending...mystically merging into the ultimate world of pure consciousness.

Is there any world of systems left that may be fitted in this speed gap? You may notice the sixth world of available god or super soul that never comes through my peel-off analysis of consciousness. It still remains untouched. This world has been given place in this model above the world of 'pure-I' and that of pure consciousness acknowledging the traditional metaphysics. The speed gap from c_4+ to 'speed tending to infinity' comes between these two worlds only. Hence, let us ascribe this speed range to the world of available God. This helps in rendering continuity to our model and filling the speed gap!

Here, I also find a subtle mutual corroboration in the concept of available god and the bizarre speed bracket (c_4+ to "speed tending to infinity") which is finite at one end and merging into infinite at the other. Concept of available god can best be understood by the account of *Ishwar* of Shankaracharya. The oxymoronic mystics of available God lies in the fact that He is someone who is fundamentally incomprehensible and inconceivable but comes under the purview of human intelligibility. It is unknown and unknowable becoming known and knowable, infinite becoming finite or say quasi-finite. The available God is the God available to the human consciousness and understanding. Human understanding cannot grasp the infinite.

Hence, the world of available God must have non-infinite and mathematically comprehensible speeds. Available God fulfills this condition very well. All speeds ascribed to this world are mathematically comprehensible including the speed tending to infinity and they are not equal to infinity.

On the other hand, the available God is nothing different from the actual God.... He is the actual God only but perceived by finite human intellect. So the available God must have all the potentiality of infinitude. In other words, the systems of the sixth world of the available God must have potential 'to go infinite'. The available God(s) fulfill(s) this condition too as the Godly systems of the sixth world are able to move at the speed 'tending to infinity' which merges into infinity at a point, may be known only to mystics but certainly not to the mathematicians!

As the system's speed goes beyond the speed tending to infinity and becomes infinity, everything becomes conceptually and mathematically incomprehensible. This can also be considered as inter-world transition from the world of available God to the world of pure consciousness (or actual God). This is where the available God identifies with pure consciousness. However philosophically, this inter-world transition is different from other transitions. This is because the available God is not different from pure consciousness. Pure consciousness is the ultimate reality. Human consciousness sees this ultimate reality as available God, which is the intelligible version of the former.

Technically, sub-infinity speeds of the systems of the sixth world of available God are like intelligible and empirical snapshots of inconceivable infinite speed captured by limited human intellect. If I stick to my *peel-off-consciousness-like-onion* analysis, I did not find the sixth level of consciousness as any separate layer. If so is true, the speed band of the systems of *Atman lok* or souls may be taken as c_3+ to 'tending to infinite' with no transition at c_4.

The available God is then fundamentally no different from pure soul. We may then assume God(s) with system speed(s) in the higher range of the same speed band and with system definitions that allow higher energy in one system. In that case, God is conscious system with larger system definitions than the individual human soul but comes in the same league as any soul.

However both ways, either we take available God as finite snapshot of infinite pure consciousness or a conscious system in same speed bracket as souls but with much larger cosmic energy than individual soul may have, He is like super soul…super enough to overwhelm and help individual souls!

With the thesis of **K**, I find all my gods running incessantly here and there in the heaven. Peace is not available even there. Nothing more tragic can happen to mankind whose gods are neither at peace with themselves nor have time to stop and listen to the trillions of prayers coming to them daily.... And if physical systems are the slowest, the earth must be the coziest place for God to take shelter!

Jampak Zu

Now an explosive question comes—If available God and its world is nothing but pure consciousness as captured and conceived by human intellect, it means the world of available God is nothing but delusion to human intellect! There are no real systems that move in the speed range of c_4+ to 'that tending to infinity'. Is this acceptable?... A world of delusion in multi-layer model of reality!!!

My turn to answer. If you go strictly by *Advaita Vedanta* of Shankaracharya, it is actually delusion.... Not only the sixth world of available God but all the lower levels up to the physical world are ultimately delusion. Anything other than pure consciousness is delusion. Though Shankar never talks of the seven layers of reality, he does differentiate between observational reality of phenomenal plane and the actual reality at the ultimate plane of pure consciousness. He claims that the world we observe and live in is real in our own reference frame i.e., in the reference frame of limited human intellect. However, as one rises to the plane of pure consciousness, this worldly plane of reality becomes unreal. Pure consciousness is the only ultimate reality and according to Shankar, everything else is ultimately unreal.

For him, reality is relative where something may be real or unreal with respect to one reference frame/world or another. Worldly phenomena are real with respect to observing human mind but ultimately unreal as human consciousness breaks its limits and becomes one with the pure consciousness. At the level of pure consciousness, which is the ultimate reality, only pure consciousness exists. Worldly phenomena turn out to be delusive. However, this cannot be experienced while standing on the phenomenal plane.

I too find reality a relative notion. My idea of relativity of reality is a bit different from the one expounded by Shankar (I doubt that I really differ). When I say that reality is relative term, I prefer to mean that telescopically something is more or less real than the other. On the scale of consciousness, the higher world is more real than the lower world with world of pure consciousness at the top, which is ultimately and absolutely real, or the most real of all the realities. So the physical world is the least real. The world of sense-level consciousness is more real than the physical world and less real than the world of mental consciousness.

For Shankar, at the level of pure consciousness everything turns out to be unreal. On reaching this level, everything else is just like the left dreams or mental images with no real existential value. I differ in opinion here.

If our physical mortal existence is just like dream to God or pure consciousness with no real value, what is the use of establishing cosmic harmony?...What is the need for God to listen to prayers? And one who does not listen is not our God.... Nothing in the grand structure of cosmic reality can be ultimately unreal even from the noumenal plane of pure consciousness. A world can only be less or very less real in comparison to higher reality. To me reality is as relative as space and time in physics.

To the student of physics, this 'relativity of reality' may look bizarre. Is it not? But the concepts of reality, consciousness and systemic speed are so inter-woven (we have seen this) that a theory of relativity if works in the field of speed must also work in the field of reality!

In my model, the least reality is ascribed to the physical world we live in, though to us it looks the most real. The reality of worldly phenomena is directly perceivable. We never see a table or a chair to be the less real than our mental consciousness of it. Their reality is visible, accessible and requires no proof. However, when I say that the table in front of me is real, no matter how forceful and compulsive the reality of table seems to me, it is me, my consciousness of senses and mind which is attributing the status of reality to the table or vindicating its status as real. Can I believe in the reality of table if my senses and mind are suggesting me contrary?... Obviously not. Hence to my consciousness, the objective and existential validity of the table comes only after my consciousness of mind and senses. Hence at least epistemologically, the existential status of table must be lower than the reality of consciousness that is authenticating and vindicating the table as [somewhat] real and hence, the physical world comes out to be less real than the mental world. Through this discussion I just wanted to bring out two points:

1. There is nothing bizarre to say that reality is relative. A thing can be more or less real than the other.

2. There is nothing bizarre in attributing less reality in the phenomena of the physical world we live in and more reality to other consciousness levels. Epistemologically, this situation is more logical and comfortable.

Now the question arises—If something is true epistemologically, will it be essentially true even ontologically? Well.... It is a philosophical issue. Reality is perceptual. If something cannot be seen as real, that thing cannot be real! Philosophically this may turn out to be a very controversial statement if one hastily jumps to conclusion. Here, I mean to say that out of the six levels of consciousness (from sense level to pure consciousness) if no level can ever see something as real, then that something is nothing. It must be absolutely unreal and null. Here the word 'can' implies potentiality or possibility of seeing.

Actual seeing is not the prerequisite or litmus of reality. Reality of a reality [real thing] lies in the fact of its potentiality of being seen as reality. Hence, the essence of reality is its knowability or possibility of its knowledge as something existing concretely [and not as mere fact of academia]. We can clearly see that ontology of reality at root becomes one with its epistemology.

Perhaps, this one-ness of ontology and epistemology also reflects the inter-weaving of reality and consciousness throughout our cosmic model of reality. Reality is the essence of existence. It represents ontology. Consciousness is the principle of knowing. It represents epistemology.

> *Ultimately, the knower and the knowledge is one*
> *and the same thing.*
>
> **Shankaracharya**

The ultimate reality that is the ultimate object of knowledge is pure consciousness, which in turn is the ultimate knower. All the lower realities are manifestations of this ultimate reality and all that we know is the part manifestation of what He knows about Himself!

God being supreme con-sciousness must be in thinking mode. I think all creation is out of His thinking...and then the creatures of this thinking start thinking back on Him. Probably, it is His way of self-refection. I do not know whether he listens to prayers or not as **K** believes without any glitch of doubt. But since thinking is a big work. He is very hard working. He is a living work-in-progress.

Jampak Zu

God, to me, it seems, is a verb
not a noun, proper or improper

RB Fuller (*'No More Seconhand God'*)

The oxymoronic mystics of available God lies in the fact that He is something who is fundamentally incomprehensible and inconceivable but comes under the purview of human intelligibility. It is something unknown and unknowable becoming known and knowable, infinite becoming finite or say quasi-finite.

Pure consciousness is the ultimate reality. Human consciousness sees this ultimate reality as available God, which is the intelligible version of the former.

Consciousness has direct correlation of proportionality with speed of system(s). So the infinite consciousness can only correspond to infinite speed .

In Godly system of pure consciousness, changes in space perception occurs at the same time with zero change in time perception.

Reality of a reality [real thing] lies in the fact of its potentiality of being seen as reality.

All that we know is a part manifestation of what God knows about Himself.

TEN

We, the Secret
...The Non-science, the Occult,
the Obscure and the True

Where doubts are taller than reply,
So many ideas nothing to buy,
I'm lost, in the darkness of knowledge,
I'm the last book, left to try.

ONCE A professor of Physics claimed on coffee that science cannot tell the truth of nature. The puzzled me asked–'why'? He announced that science and truth are characteristically different. They are so different that science cannot carry the truths of nature. He continued that science is like religion!... very verbose, open and elaborate, demanding loyalty, proving, disproving, claiming, asserting, bullying by nature...and real truth is like pearl in shell...closed, un-claiming, nascent, like glimpse of revelation, and always beyond verbose arrangements of proof. It was quite poetic of him.

I always believe that if a scientist turns philosopher or a poet, he turns out better than a regular one. The coffee speech of professor reminded me of the dreams I had seen in my teenage and early youth. The secret book of nature opens up rarely and that too when you are asleep. The real truth is not in the books of science. These books are just records of perceived uniformity or pattern of things in nature noted by awake minds. So to know the truth...you have to sleep!

Jampak Zu

In the recorded history of mankind, nowhere has sleep been labelled as so sacred. Sages suggest having awake and aware mind for receiving knowledge. We grow reading mantra of '*utrishtha, jagrat, prapya varatribodhya*t', which means 'get up, wake up and achieve which should be achieved'. Now **K** wants to turn the traditional wisdom topsy-turvy. If you want to achieve knowledge, the new age mantra is, 'retire yourself in bed, sleep tight and you will achieve all the knowledge you want'.... And never ever use your mind to gain knowledge.

Mind is incapable of knowing the infinite truth. You cannot put the infinite in a small bowl. Real truth is fluid and poetic. It can be known either through the heart or the soul. Mind is the biggest gap between you and the divine truth. It is like a mirror which reflects your gross existence and hides your inner self or real existence. Your innermost conscious core...your soul is the real you. Mind engages your real consciousness with so much fleeting data of gross existence that your consciousness forgets to acknowledge itself. To know the self is self-realization. However, for this to happen you have to switch off your nasty mind. You have to disengage your core consciousness from the flow of data and ideas processed and presented by mind. This is true meditation. Meditation is not the focus of mind rather it is annihilation of mind.

We are unable to know God because our mind is all-powerful. It filters all the ideas as rational and irrational according to its own training and growth and only accepts the rational. To our mind, knowledge can only be rational. I think the ultimate truths of nature are irrational, poetic and beyond mediocrity of certitude and fixity.

At the core of it, knowledge is mystical. If the source of all being has infinite uncertainty of Heisenberg's type; if it is all so much gray, why to expect differentiative clarity in the field of knowledge? To know is not to know. If you know with certitude, this is one sure sign that you do not know fully. Ultimate truths and ultimate knowledge are not like rational concrete facts to be just known by mind. They are mystical enlightenments to be felt by higher consciousness when they pop up inside as divine favour. I realize He appears in the realm of ignorance as mystical revelation. He does not prefer rational appearances in the realm of probing human mind. For Him, our cloudy sub-conscious is a safer landing. I may model Him taking clues from Physics only to an extent as He reveals Himself in mystical ways. Beyond that all fails.

The path of true knowledge is spiritual in nature. Spirituality means many things. Its path is a path of mystical ignorance and wonder. Universe is ultimately mystical and indescribable in terms of human intellect and spirituality lies in seeing its mystical essence without seeking any answer or explanation. It is in non-fixation of ideas and concepts and also in peace and fullness of thoughts. Spirituality is in celebration of surrendering your mind in search of the ultimate truth.

To see something without knowing it through compulsive universal rationality of human mind is a way of spirituality. It is just seeing with mystery...this is *darshan* and not philosophy or love for knowledge...it is just love for seeing. Every piece of knowledge is a determination and hence is a limitation. Knowledge with claim or certainty is a limitation. Ignorance is limitlessness. You can reach God not by claiming knowledge but by mystical ignorance. Every norm, form, value and pattern that man or material follows or adopts, comes with its own set of determination and limitation.

Aspiration for knowledge is the result of natural human inclination to know and decipher the patterns and probabilities out of chaos and randomness. Mind wants to discern some order out of natural chaos. The models of order which explain and predict the processes of nature and society become the pieces of human knowledge. Anything that falls out of the model turns either an exception or a miracle, depending upon the magnitude of deviance. So knowledge gets an umbilical relation with predictability. However, predictability is a statistical determination; hence a type of limitation. Higher the predictability, lesser is the wonder and so is the spirituality. Thus, knowledge and values which symbolize fixation of patterns are the biggest obstacle in the path of spirituality. The golden path of spiritual life goes through unlearning the learnt knowledge and values. A soul and mind encumbered with claimable knowledge and values cannot be called 'enlightened and liberated one'.

Spirituality is a perspective, a way of thinking, a way of life that provokes and then permeates in the process of self-search and self-evolution. Spirituality has nothing to do with renunciation of the worldly; it can parallel with rejoicing. Spirituality itself is a type of rejoicing at a higher plane. It is a celebration of the mystery of existence. It is harmony with the enigma of universe.

Science is the murderer of mystery.

Osho

I think it only makes an attempt to murder the mystery. Science only discovers the procedural aspect of universe. It never captures the substantive and just answers the methodological how and why without penetrating into the philosophical what.

The world is full of things and thoughts, people and colours. Can we really describe the entire world in terms of atoms and subatomic particles that make it? We may partly describe things but cannot describe thoughts. Ideas are not made of atoms. Colours are not made of atoms either. Can we even describe things or physical objects fully? The answer is —No. We even do not know what is this matter-energy that makes atoms or subatomic particles and from where matter and other non-matter has come. We only see them, not their source. We only capture effects and not the cause. Fullness of universe shows itself in bits and pieces. The more I go inside myself, the more strongly I realize that we only see the snapshots of reality and not the whole picture. We do not know the foundation, source and elemental meaning of existence. All the existence is mystery to us. To search for an answer of this mystery, is science. To believe in some answer without knowing it, is religion. To believe that there is no answer is 'atheism'. To realize that this mystery itself can be celebrated as answer and does not require any further rational answer is 'spirituality'.

Why a mystery should at all be explored for an answer? Can we not live with it? The answer can be both positive and negative. Actually, mind always wants to have a worldview where everything stands explained, where everything is settled in a web of cause and effect. A mystery does not fit in such worldview. So it perturbs the mind and gives a kind of intellectual unease.

Probably, we are yet to realize that mystery is the integral character of objects and observations. Our mind is constrained by certain programmed ways of perceiving and understanding. We see things around but do not know what Kant calls 'things-in-themselves'. When you see an apple, what actually you see is certain combination of colours, tactile properties, shape, weight, taste, etc. All these are data for mind. The world around is a big data base for mind. Does all that we see actually exist or is it just 'data-in-mind' or 'data-in-consciousness'?..we do not know. We know things to the extent we see them. It is all at the border of knowing and not-knowing. Conceivably, everything is also at the border of being and not-being. So all the phenomenal existence has been described by *Vedanta* as *maya* or delusion. *Maya* is God...partially captured by our limited mind. When known fully, it is only God and no *maya*. It is non-existent manifestation of the existent. The only existent is God. There is no cause-effect relation in God and *maya*, for in reality, there is no effect existing separately from cause. *Maya* or the entire world around is thus at the saddle point balance between existence and non-existence. This existential status of *maya* or the 'world-as-we-see' is mysterious to our limited mind.

The world is not mysterious because we do not know it fully. Not knowing something is just crude ignorance. Mystery is different from such ignorance. Mystery carries with itself some sort of irrationality and absence of logic and clue. To be between existence and non-existence is incomprehensible to our rational mind...hence, it is irrational...and hence, it is a mystery.

Usually, we get so much familiar with the world around that it seizes to seem a mystery. We see the trees and birds, rivers and mountains, buildings and people in our day-to-day life so frequently and unquestioningly that their presence rarely intrigues us. We take them for granted. However, the entire world we see is a mystery that our familiarity with this world cannot take away. Mystery is absence of explanation, absence of answer and possibility of it, absence of foundational and essential meaning of rational type and not the absence of familiarity. Mystery and familiarity can coexist.

God is a narrative mystery—the ultimate reservoir of mystery. We narrate God as explanation of all foundational problems of existence, as answers to questions that cannot be answered, rationally; from where this universe and its matter has come into existence, what life is made of and why there is life, is there any controlling power of universe, is everything predestined, if all the colours appear in the eyes only, is the world actually colourless, why there is sorrow and happiness, etc. Every possible answer to such questions raises further many questions than it answers, and the chain of questions and answers invariably come to a dead end; call it God or fate or nature, whatever you may like, depending on your socially declared degree of theism or atheism. Just as the various rivers and rivulets pour into the sea, which is the ultimate reservoir of water, the mysteries attached to numerous components and aspects of this world pour into God in search for an answer.

Mystery is a non-answer. God is a mega non-answer. God never answers to the queries of inquisitive mind. He never dispels His own or any other mystery. He is a point of no return. After knowing God, mind stops questioning. It does not mean that it gets all the answers after knowing God. It only means that the questions themselves disappear along with the questioning mind.

So the secret to spiritual way of living and thinking is rediscovering the mystery spread all around and inside;

rejoicing, wondering and celebrating it. It is like surprising the obvious. There is nothing in this world that can be explained ultimately. All the gurus of religion and science tend to answer things...not bad, but many of them fail to appreciate the essential nature of creation when they claim certitude and authority in their answers. This world can only be explained illusively and superficially by an obsessively and genetically simplistic mind. To fully understand this world or any facet of it is a sure shot symptom of not understanding it.

His Holiness, Reverend **K**! Thanks for your sermon on whatever mount you are sitting upon. If I say with claim that I agree with you, you will say this is the surest sign that you have not understood me. If I say that I do not agree with you, I fear that you may give another sermon. So I am at the saddle point balance between agreement and disagreement with you. And believe me, I am celebrating this irrational non-conclusiveness for the first time in my life! I have no other option. But one thing I can claim with all the certitude of visible and invisible universe that whatever you have discoursed in last few pages is not 'Physics of God' or devil. Will you be in full rational agreement with this?

Jampak Zu

I fully accept the point of Jampak Zu that this is not Physics. But what I dealt in my core exposition in earlier chapters was not physics either—at least in puristic perspective of science as there was no experiment and no proof! It is an extrapolation of our understanding of the visible physical world through Physics into the possible realm of invisible metaphysical reality.

I only want to bring out my personal realization that the secrets of nature are presented to us in ajar envelop of obscurity. It only gives its own glimpses. Probably, God is tempted to signal the mankind that we still have long way to discover the best-kept secrets of the universe and Himself.

I was reading a folklore somewhere, which goes thus:

> When God created the universe and human being, he made the human mind was very intelligent, inquisitive and probing, even more than what He had initially planned for. It had huge capacity to discover truths, create ideas and connect things. God did not want that human mind should ever know the master plan of His creation. But He was unable to find any place where human mind could not reach to hide His master plan. Then an angel came to God and asked the reason for His worry. God told him that He had mistakenly made the human mind very intelligent and there was no place in universe where human mind could not reach in due course of time. He wanted to hide all the secret truths of His creation from man. The angel advised God that the best place to keep the secrets of universe is the inside of man himself—deep inside the human mind. The mind is so objective and restlessly outward looking that it does never see inside itself. God then put all the treasure of cosmic secret in the depths of human consciousness. He also realized that this

was also a very good hide for Himself too. So the God too along with His heavenly paraphernalia slipped into the deepest layers of human consciousness. And the intelligent and silly human mind is still searching the God and the secret. The best-kept secret is kept just inside.

This story is more telling than what it tells. All the natural sciences including Physics are objective. They see the outward story. They see what is shown. They never see the observer. They never see He who is seeing. It is not on the agenda of Physics. And thus, it misses the secret.

I think to categorize knowledge and process of knowledge in watertight compartments of outwardly and inwardly; objective and subjective is not good. Physics is outwardly not concerned with 'He who sees'. Spirituality is all the search of this inside 'He who sees'. So, the two may seem opposite. However, the very thesis proposed by **K** shows the physical world as the first layer in multi-layered structure of reality. All the other layers are just different levels of human consciousness only. This whole thesis moves from physical to metaphysical, from physics to spirituality. If spirituality is a quest for our own inner consciousness, the quest for inside 'He who sees', this model renders Physics the first natural stepping-stone in the path of spirituality. And once Physics becomes the part of 'project-search-God', the first chapter of

Jampak Zu

divine secrets we start using the vocabulary of Physics to describe the cosmic reality. This is exactly what **K** has done. He has used the language of Physics to know and discuss God. It is not bringing God in the ambit of Physics; rather bringing Physics in the ambit of God. The project of K is not all about rendering the God more comprehensible and clear...it is about rendering the physics more obscure too.

It is so positive to see Physics as the starting point of spiritual understanding. It dilutes the thematic antagonism between the two. The journey to inner self starts from our objective outwardly-ness. We know our subtle existences by first knowing our gross physical existence.

I would like to discuss two very important concepts, which may look too religious or obscure to some readers. First is the theory of karma as propounded in Jainism and second is the concept of *chakras* in human body.

Jainism as philosophy had never appealed to me. When I first read the concept of karma as propounded by Mahavir Swami, I was highly unimpressed. He says that karma is like matter which sticks to your soul like particles of dirt. In order to reclaim your true self, you have to get rid of the sticky particles of karma clinging to your soul. I found this description too childish. It was as if Mahavir Swami was trying to make understand a crowd of low IQ religious devotees in simple figurative manner referring karma as dirt particles to be washed away. To me, the idea of karmic matter sticking to soul was like mythological symbolism and religious picturesque for consumption of unquestioning minds. I never realized its import and depth before deciphering my own dreams.

The thesis we have discussed about cosmic reality starts with this physical world. To recapitulate, this world is made up of all the systems which may have speed range between zero to that of light in free space denoted by 'c'. Usage of the term 'system' is generic. By system I mean any body, no matter how big it may be, or any particle, no matter how tiny it may be. From galaxies, stars, planets to tennis balls, tables and chairs and then dust particles, atoms, subatomic particles, photons, quarks or Higgs bosons—all are systems. You can define anything as system and choose its own boundaries as per definition. We have also discussed that a moving body or particle has all the properties of wave and hence is equivalent to a wave and vice versa. Physics calls it 'wave-particle duality'. So a moving or standing wave is also a system. A selected piece of electromagnetic wave is a system. We have also seen that every physical system is made of mass-energy, and every matter is energy and all energy is matter i.e., mass and energy are one and the same thing.

Hence, it is not correct to say that systems are made up of mass and energy as per the grammar of Physics. Better say that systems are made of mass-energy. Mass-energy is the elemental substance of this world. So what is common sensically, taken as form of energy like heat and light is matter too. Light is an electromagnetic wave and it also has matter. It has all the qualities of gross matter and is affected by gravitational force too.

As we translate from the physical world to the non-physical world, we actually start dealing with systems with speeds higher than the speed of light in free space. They are non-physical systems, very fine wave-particles moving with incomprehensible speeds. We call them non-physical owing to their speed and fineness as they cannot be contained by the space-time continua of physical world and hence are incomprehensible and invisible to human minds. However, they are after all extremely tiny wave-particles of very high energy and speed. So they also have matter-energy. The only difference is that their matter-energy is non-physical as it cannot be captured and measured physically.

We can understand this by rough analogy of electro-magnetic spectrum. Human eyes can only capture some portion of this spectrum seen as the light of seven colours. The visible light is nothing but electromagnetic wave whose frequency falls in that portion. As the frequency goes below the frequency of red light or above the frequency of violet light, the human eyes stop seeing them. It does not mean that waves of frequency lesser than red or higher than violet do not exist. They exist and are captured by other means but not by human eyes. Similarly, there exist very fine wave-particles of high energy, moving faster than the speed of light in free space. However, they do not exist for physical world and its physics as normal human mind encumbered with gross body is unable to capture them, just like human eyes are incapable of capturing infrared or ultraviolet rays. We need very different ways to capture the non-physical reality. And here, it comes in spiritual ways.

We have seen that there are various levels of consciousness. As we translate to higher levels of consciousness, the fineness, the energy and the speed of systems go on increasing. The substance of sense-level consciousness is just high energy wave particles that are faster, finer and subtler than the mass-energy of gross physical world. Similarly, the building blocks of mental consciousness are also nothing but wave-particles that are more energetic, faster, finer and subtler than systems of sense-level consciousness and so on. However, the bottom line is that everything is and can be analysed into wave-particles having physical or non-physical energy-matter. Even the various layers of human consciousness and its content are made up of some material and some system. This picture of cosmic reality is astonishingly drossy and materialistic. Every emotion or idea or concept is just a quantum or form or disturbance at some or the other level of consciousness. So every thought, feeling and realization is theoretically describable in terms of some alchemy of wave-particles.

'Theory of karma' is largely understood or misunderstood as obscure balance sheet of good and bad actions for individuals. Sages of various religions preach that God sees our actions and we reap fruits of our good or bad past karmas. However, the Jainism's understanding of karma goes beyond the crude arithmetic of our actions. Every thought, speech or action, which can leave impression on our soul is 'karma'. Every thought, speech and action is a disturbance in the still field of consciousness. A disturbance is wave. Wave is a particle too. It is an envelope of matter and energy. So when

Mahavir Swami says that particles of karma sticks to our soul and we get our true self when we get rid of this karmic dross, he is true. To what I had initially thought as symbolic myth turned out to be the precise truth of the nature in my understanding and personal revelation of the divine secret. To me, Mahavir Swami was a scientist of the highest order who experimented with his own consciousness.

Soul or 'pure-I' as I have called it in my thesis is itself a system, extremely subtle and conscious. Soul is the deepest and most authentic address of human individuality. It is a pie of pure consciousness, a quantum of extremely fine non-physical energy. Soul is atomic. It means it cannot be further cut into pieces or smaller subsystems. It is not made up of smaller systems or particles. It is basic and pure element of cosmic reality. Every sentient being has a soul. The ultimate purpose of life is to know your true self, your soul. But soul itself is the knower or observer. So the goal of life is to know the knower. Soul is like a luminous electric bulb. The lower layers of human existence i.e., body, senses, mind and intellect-ego are karmic depositions only. They cover the bulb of soul as mud. These depositions do not let the true nature of soul flow out of it. We have to clear the mud deposited on the ever-lit bulb of soul so that the light will automatically follow.

Bhagvat Gita describes soul as indestructible. It is so because it is atomic. The usage of this word atomic is literal. 'Atom' means something that cannot be divided further. All the depositions on soul are destructible because the systems of lower four worlds (physical, sense-level consciousness, mental consciousness and 'pure–I') are not atomic. They are made of subsystems. Hence, they can be decomposed into their components. A soul being the basic and pure element of cosmos cannot be divided or decomposed into pieces. It is the basic unit of consciousness, energy and existence. Hence, it is indestructible. Souls constitute their own world shown as the fifth level of reality in my thesis.

Now, I would also like to discuss the seven *chakras* of human body and the idea of *kundalini* power, which rests in lowest *chakra* and goes through all the *chakras* when awakened.

Jainism does not go beyond soul. However, we have seen that this thesis traverses two more levels of reality, *Anupadak lok* or the 'world of available God' and *Adi lok* or the 'world of infinite pure consciousness'.

Thus, there are seven worlds or seven layers of cosmic existence based on the speed and the fineness of systems, value of Planck's constant and degree of Heisenberg's uncertainty principle and so on. A human existence participates in all the seven worlds simultaneously. We are multi-layered beings. Our gross physical body is our participation in the physical world. We have subtler bodies too whose substances belong to the higher worlds. Thus, human beings contain the seven bodies or *kosh* or *karan* corresponding to the seven worlds. These seven bodies are like layers of an onion. We have to peel them off one by one in the process of self-realization in order to reach at its core. There is surprising match in the numbers of levels of reality and numbers of *chakras* in human body. As I went deep, it was not just a quantitative coincidence but there appeared qualitative one-to-one correspondence between the *chakras* and the levels of reality. This correspondence is mysteriously simple.

After physics, philosophy and religious sermons, let us now study some biology. Who says it is 'Physics of God?' It is 'all disciplines on everything', landing up on nothing!

Jampak Zu

Before we ponder upon this correspondence, I must brief my readers about the science and mystics of *chakras*. *Chakras* are described as energy centres in the body. They are understood to feed the different organs of body with life force and vitality.

The seven *chakras* are aligned along the vertebral column and head. Five *chakras* out of seven are placed on the vertebral column and two are above, in the head. These are illustrated in the Figure 10.1.

Muladhara Chakra

This *chakra* is placed two fingers above the anus, at the end of spine, below the sacrum bone. *Mula* means 'root' and *adhara* means 'support'. According to yogis, as the name suggests, it is the base support of all the life energies

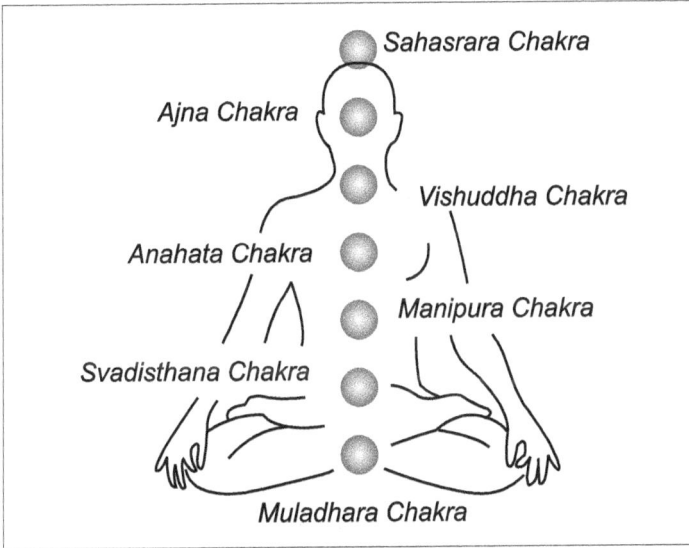

Fig. 10.1 Seven Major *Chakras*

of human beings. This divine energy called *Kundalini* is understood to be laying idle on this *chakra*. Through Pranayama and meditation, this hidden energy can be drawn upward to higher *chakras*.

At gross level, this *chakra* is said to nourish excretory organs, pelvic area and partly the sex organs. Despite having a specific physical location in human body, this *chakra* represents the gross existence of human being which is nothing but this physical body. This *chakra* is the representation of the participation of human existence in the physical world in form of physical body. Hence, this *chakra* is the centre of all the physical matter-energy, which makes a human body and also the repository of all the subtle but dormant non-physical energy this physical human body unknowingly carries. This sleeping non-physical energy supported by the gross body is represented by *Kundalini*.

Svadisthana Chakra

This *chakra* is situated on the spinal cord behind the regenerative organs. At physical level, it nourishes liver, spleen, kidneys and partly the sex organs.

However, this *chakra* is the representation of the human existence's participation in the world of sense-level consciousness or the 'astral world' as it is called in theosophy. Hence, this *chakra* is the 'centre of the astral body' or *Bhuvah kosh* in similar way as *Muladhara chakra* is the centre of our physical body. This chakra controls all our astral substance or the non-physical matter-energy belonging to the astral world.

Ayurveda, the ancient school of medicine, calls this astral substance as *prana* or 'life energy'. This astral substance is also called 'etheric substance' in theosophical literatures, *chi* or *qi* in Chinese literature; *prana*, *ojas* or *tejas* in Indian scriptures; *pnuema* in Greek scriptures; and so on and so forth. It is the substance of existence of life, it is the elixir of life. It spreads throughout the body and nourishes it. It also spreads beyond body in the whole universe, nourishing and maintaining it. In the cosmic field of *prana* or astral substance, we are localized bundle or envelope of *prana* where the physical matter is organized according to the principles of life. Matter is energy and energy is matter. If *prana* is energy, it has to be matter too. *Prana* is actually very fine high-energy fluid matter with overt primal consciousness. Through *prana*, we are invisibly connected with the entire universe, physical and non-physical, visible and invisible. It gives us élan vital—life force, health, beauty, vigour, calmness and aesthetic propensities and enhanced creative sense. *Prana* is basically energy, a non-physical energy, that means it is not the element of this physical world, and is beyond the physical world and the reach of physics.

Ayurveda describes that there are thousands of invisible *nadis* in human body through which the luminous and fluid astral substance flows throughout the body. Of them, there are 15 main *nadis*. Out of these 15 *nadis*; *Ida, Pingla* and *Sushumna* are of utmost importance. They are the invisible astral channels in which *prana* flows, just like the blood that flows in visible veins and arteries.

There are many types of astral substances. Only that which flows in the body is known as *prana*. However, astral substance spreads everywhere. Even in body, *prana* has many categorizations. The *prana* that flows upward through vertebral column is called *ojas*. The *prana* that accumulates above *Vishuddha chakra* i.e., on the face and outermost surface of the gross body (skin) is called *tejas*. In the normal body functioning there are five kinds of *prana* involved:

Apana Prana

Apana prana is located from the navel to the big toe. It helps in the elimination of all waste material from the body effectively and keeps the body free of diseases.

Samana Prana

This resides between the heart and the navel region. *Samana prana* keeps our digestive system healthy. It activates the digestive juices and is responsible for assimilation and distribution of nutrients in our food.

Prana

It is placed between the throat and the heart. It maintains the heartbeat and breathing and is responsible for all the oxygen exchange between the lungs and the outside air.

Udana Prana

This *prana* is located between head (skull) and throat. Healthy condition of this *prana* prevents cold and cough. Some yogis claim that at the moment of death, *Udana prana* carries away with it the karmas of many previous lives deposited in our subtle bodies.

Vyana Prana

This *prana* circulates with the blood in the whole body.

Manipura Chakra

This *chakra* is located just behind the back of the navel on the spinal column. At physical level, this *chakra* nourishes the stomach, digestive system, especially the intestine and a part of liver.

Despite its physical locale and area of control, this *chakra* basically represents the participation of human existence in the world of mental consciousness. So *Manipura chakra* corresponds to our *Manomaya kosh* or 'mental body'—the body made up of non-physical matter-energy of the world of mental consciousness. This *chakra* controls all the mental energy of human being.

All the mental awareness, calmness, chaos or order of thoughts, fleeting feelings of satisfaction or restlessness, generosity or otherwise, are governed by this *chakra*. Since this *chakra* feeds our digestive system at physical level, it is said that mental anxiety or disturbance has direct bearing upon our digestive system. Any mental disturbance may trigger malfunctioning of *Manipura chakra*, which may be immediately manifested as loss of appetite, constipation or loose bowels.

Anahata Chakra

This *chakra* is placed on the spinal column behind the heart and the sternum bone. This is also known as 'heart *chakra*'. At physical level, it nourishes the heart and the surrounding area.

This *chakra* represents the participation of human existence in the world of 'I-ness' or ego. This is also called the 'world of intellect' or *pragya*. So *Anhata chakra* is the centre of all the subtle and fine non-physical matter-energy in us that belongs to the fourth level of consciousness and which constitutes *Vijyanmaya kosh* or *Aham kosh* or the subtle body of ego and intellect in us. This chakra controls all our perception of self or I-ness and intellect associated with it. This chakra carries our self-perception and self-identity. It also controls all our understanding, wisdom and stable feelings of devotion, joy and love.

According to *Upanishads*, meditation on *Anahata chakra* establishes the heart in God by generating devotion and love for Him. A heart breaking news or sudden loss of joy or love creates malfunctioning in *Anahat chakra* and since this *chakra* feeds heart physically, one may feel physical pinch in the heart area in such situations. It may also lead to a heart attack if this *chakra* is very weak and has weakened the heart over a period of time.

Vishuddha Chakra

This *chakra* is placed on the spinal column at the back of throat. At physical level, it feeds cervical area, throat, arms, eyes, lower parts of face including mouth, tongue, ears and nose. This way it nourishes all the five sense organs.

It represents the participation of human existence in the world of 'pure-I' or souls. So, it is the centre of all the subtle energy that belongs to the fifth level of consciousness. It corresponds to *Atma kosh* or *Anandamaya kosh* or 'soul'.

This *chakra* controls all the attachments and detachments. It controls attachments because it feeds all the sense organs through which human being communicates and engages with the outer physical world. However, as it corresponds to soul, which is the purest state of self devoid of all karmic attachments, it also resonates the feeling of detachment. This dialectic role of *Vishuddha chakra* renders it a unique position in spiritual evolution. From *Vishuddha chakra* upward, the spiritual channel is extremely complicated. The next *Ajna chakra* is not just a simple succession of *chakra* counting. A lot happens in between. However, it is too obscure to be the part of this book.

The content of this book has already and unexpectedly turned so obscure that **K** should not shy away from it. If he is allowed to write more chapters, I believe he will also cover some black magic! So as co-author of this book I veto against any more chapter in this book. If he is not writing the full story on *Vishuddha chakra* and connectivity between *Vishuddha* and *Ajna chakra*, one possible reason may be his own inability to decipher his so-called 'dreams of revelation' for such deep levels of consciousness. He may be unable to meditate at such high level. I think his confidence is shaking in asserting truths.

Jampak Zu

To answer the doubts of my colleague, I would like to say both—Yes and No. That I am unable to meditate with differentiative clarity to single out *Vishuddha chakra* and to see the energy channel between *Vishuddha* and *Ajna chakra* is true. However, deciphered dreams are crystal clear and I am relying on them in my exposition. The complicated nature of *Vishuddha chakra* and upward route to *Ajna chakra* onward is not at all required to be dealt here.

The discussion on *chakras* is incorporated in this book

only to show the natural correspondence between the levels of reality brought out earlier and *chakras* in our body. It helps understand the multi-layered existence of human being across the seven levels of consciousness.

There may be a lot of confusions and curiosities in some readers about *chakras*, their origin, import and significance. However, despite temptation on discussing in details, I would like to bring to Jampak's attention that this is not the book on *chakras*.

Ajna Chakra

This *chakra* is located in the middle of the forehead, just above the eyebrows and two fingers inside. It comes almost close to the centre of brain.

This *chakra* represents the participation of human existence in the 'world of God or super souls' or *Anupadak lok*. It symbolizes the presence of God in human beings. On its activation, our destiny follows from our will.

At the level of *Vishuddha chakra* activation, we become the participant of cosmic alchemy. However, at the level of *Ajna chakra* activation, we are the alchemist.

Sahasrara Chakra

This *chakra* is placed above the *brahmarandhra* in the limbic area. It is at the top of the head when our eyes see straight at right angle to the length of our body. This is the last and topmost *chakra* and represents infinite pure consciousness.

It is the state of bliss, the ultimate truth, the ultimate object of knowledge, the ultimate inside knower and the ultimate inside, He who sees, the ultimate witness. At this level, knowledge and knower are one. Meditation on this *chakra* gives blissful delight. The complete activation of this *chakra* is nothing but 'nirvana'. At this level, consciousness goes beyond cosmic alchemy. It denotes pure blissful consciousness devoid of any form.

In a human body, *Sahasrara chakra* is encumbered with the other six layers of various types of matter-energy, which are successively coarser and slower than pure consciousness. It must be noted that neither *Ajna chakra* nor *Sahasrara chakra*, in the state they are physically located in the human body, are themselves God or pure consciousness. These *chakras* are locations of divinity, which successively appear as they get unburdened by lower bodies. These two *chakras* themselves become divine when they stand alone without lower bodies—and when so happens, they cease to be *chakras* of human body as there remains no body and no human identity or individuality.

Call it obscureness or enlightenment, the ancient oriental wisdom of the seven *chakras* corroborates the thesis of seven levels of existence and consciousness and also the axiom that human existence is multi-layered owing to its participation in all the seven worlds.

All the secrets of cosmos and divinity are inside us. We ourselves are the secret. We are the elixir of life. The God and devil are inside. We are the answers to all the questions this world poses to us. What we see and know through science, logic, religion, superstition, philosophy and art is all perception. The substance is inside us. The whole world as we see is symbolic. It is just a representation or reflection of some higher reality.

Every natural fact is a symbol of some spiritual fact.

R W Emerson

Jampak Zu

If my physical existence is just a symbol, I do not know what is my spiritual fact? I never found worth to see inside myself. I was never taught this either. I do not know what this self is. I always saw self as perception of perception. I do not know if the self is substantive as **K** claims. However, I do think there is something fundamentally wrong in the way we usually approach the world and understand it. All the worldly knowledge of science, psychology and philosophy being the product of mind tend to be objective. Objectivity is taken as the touchstone of fineness of any knowledge system. It is exactitude, concreteness, universal visibility and verifiability that attribute supposed superiority to objective knowledge system. Even the best of philosophies and religious discourses tend to be objective when they objectify the sacred through symbols, unroll elaborate stories of mythologies and orthodox processes of prayers, etc.

I think it is a big mistake. This misplaced emphasis on objectivity stuns the subjective evolution of consciousness through worldly experiences. Our inside remains untrained and uneducated. Unfortunately, all the critical moments of human existence that deal with extreme emotions show their presence in the domain of subjective awareness, while all the so-called certain and reliable knowledge and learning is available in the domain of objective awareness. So no good knowledge or guidance is available for help when we need it the most! So let there be great literatures, books, manuals—written and unwritten and loads of traditions representing righteousness of conformist type. Nothing answers who am I, and nothing helps when I am at crossroads!!!

We should first see the natural and cosmic literature inside us. We need to open up the shell of our own awareness. There is something written...faded and unclear. This is the divine script in all of us. We should try to read it. The more we read, clearer it will become. Unlike objective knowledge that requires a lot of words, it just requires silence. Unlike objective knowledge that proceeds and develops through questions and answers, it develops through wonder. Questions and answers throw the vague and subjective inner stuff of feeling in the domain of objective and rational cruelty where the stuff is made 'known', but not 'felt'. The structure of our rational mind blocks this divine script for its irrationality and vagueness. We forget that the secret is irrational.

We are not monolithic. There are many sentient entities inside us—many layers of consciousness working in synchrony. The higher we go, the more we move on the scale of irrationality and uncertainty. The more the rational

'I' dissolves, the more the irrational 'I' evolves. At the end of spiritual growth, we ourselves are the irrational divinity.

The path of spirituality is the path where we awake the dormant forces in us, allow them to push us to the edge, to overwhelm us to the extent we cease to exist and...then we rediscover ourself in our own absence.

Someone has said that we are endless conglomerate of awareness. We are not the singular self. We are a corporation. The more I listen to **K**, the more I fear it may be true!!!

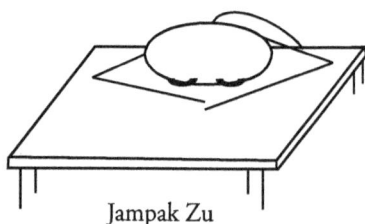

Jampak Zu

All the science and religion to guide,
All the knowledge by my side,

One night He came, and gave me a look;
Just one moment, that's all He took;

To tell that world is a curtain for show,
To laugh, to weep but not to know,

That mind has learnt, no meaning but diction;
And the truth inside is stranger than fiction.

A human existence participates in all the seven worlds simultaneously. We are multi-layered beings. Our gross physical body is our participation in the physical world. We have subtler bodies too whose substances belong to higher worlds. Thus, human beings contain seven bodies or kosh or karan corresponding to the seven worlds.

In the cosmic field of prana or astral substance, we are localized bundle or envelope of prana where the physical matter is organized according to the principles of life.

To know is not to know. If you know with certitude, this is one sure sign that you do not know fully.

To search for an answer of the mystery of existensce, is science. To believe in some answer without knowing it, is religion. To believe that there is no answer, is atheism. To realize that this mystery itself can be celebrated as answer and does not require any further rational answer, is spirituality.

www.ingramcontent.com/pod-product-compliance
Lightning Source LLC
Chambersburg PA
CBHW022123080426
42734CB00006B/231